CONNECTIONS WITH NATURE

50 moments of meeting the wild

CONNECTIONS
WITH NATURE

50 moments of meeting the wild

Compiled and edited by Kate Stephenson

First published in the UK in September 2021 by
Journey Books, an imprint of Bradt Guides Ltd
31a High Street, Chesham, Buckinghamshire, HP5 1BW, England
www.bradtguides.com

British Library Cataloguing in Publication Data
A catalogue record for this book is available from the British Library
Printed in the UK by Jellyfish Print Solutions

To find out more about our Journey Books imprint, visit www.bradtguides.com/
journeybooks

Dedicated to Ada and William
May your connection with nature remain strong
your whole life through

CONTENTS

PART TWO: EVOLVING PERSPECTIVES

PART THREE: LIFELONG CONNECTIONS

PREFACE

Back in January 2020, ahead of the most life-changing of events that many of us would ever face – and certainly the most life-changing that we have all faced collectively – an extraordinary thing happened.

I entered a travel-writing competition centred around ethical tourism – and the judges selected me as a prize winner! Literally days after leaving my job at *National Geographic Kids* magazine to venture into the world of freelance writing (can you imagine now how poorly timed that decision was?!), I had landed the most amazing start – an award; some writing publicity; and most unbelievably: a trip of a lifetime to Costa Rica and the Peruvian Amazon to experience ethical travel tours that would introduce me to sloths for the first time, see me staying in fabulous ecolodges, enjoying birdwatching tours and many other exciting plans. Which, of course, I would write about. I planned, prepped and saved – as with many of these competition prizes, the cost of the flights was not included.

Fast-forward two months and we all know the story. The world was shut down and the realisation that I'd left a steady and successful career to become a freelancer at a time when no-one could take the risk of using their finances to commission any outside work, was beginning to hit home. The idea of taking any kind of exotic trip turned into a cruel joke.

Never one to be beaten, I decided that now would be a great time for two things: an online support network of like-minded people; and the chance to feel like a valued professional again. A stay-at-home freelancer that wasn't freelancing just wouldn't cut it for me.

And so, the idea of The Wildlife Blogger Crowd was born.

A 'crowd' and not a 'club', the community was named to give a sense of levelling out. A club raised connotations of exclusivity, membership fees and hierarchy; a crowd symbolised the collective: infinite in its ability to grow, yet still each individual remains equal in status and decidedly as valuable in raising the collective voice. The more we stand and speak together, the greater the strength of the crowd.

After 10 years of blogging, and constantly reaffirming the power of storytelling, my vision for The Wildlife Blogger Crowd came from a desire to create a Wildlife & Nature Blog Community dedicated to supporting one another, sharing articles, organising collaborations, asking questions, and seeking brand opportunities. The platform was designed as a positive and safe space for wildlife and nature bloggers to share posts, join discussions and support other content creators.

As our community grew and connections between members became stronger, plans for a free mentoring scheme developed; and then the 'holy grail' of a printed book crossed my mind. A chance to give every single one of this talented community the chance to list themselves as a published writer.

Well, thoughts that run across my mind have the uncanny ability to get stuck there. Six months after launching The Wildlife Blogger Crowd, and too many weeks of Covid-19 restrictions to even differentiate between the months anymore; I thought about those savings accrued for my flights to South America – and I put them all into creating this book.

Staying grounded (quite literally – and figuratively too, as it would happen) at the beginning of this new stage of my career had changed my perception; and building up the opportunities available to my beloved online community now seemed more far important than chasing those that I would keep to myself.

If I could not get out there and explore the world, enjoy its natureful offerings and write about it, then I would bring the world to me, share in other people's natureful experiences and create a book out of it! Hopefully one that will inspire all of the members of our collective blogger crowd, and beyond.

When I tasked members of the crowd with the incredibly open brief of sharing their most memorable connections with nature – to be submitted in whichever medium they were most comfortable working in (i.e. blog post-style, poetry, prose, art or photography) – I knew there was a risk that it may not 'fit together' in the way that one would expect of a book.

If my days working as a magazine editor taught me anything, it's that readers like to be taken on a narrative journey – even if they don't always realise that it's happening. Even a seemingly random collection of articles and images must somehow flow, in order to please the unconscious mind.

Nonetheless, it was a risk worth taking. I wanted the genuine thing; I wanted our crowd of wordsmiths and visual storytellers to share their truths; their passionate and unrestricted tales of connections with nature.

When it came to it, searching for a thread to weave each piece together actually came quite easily; from connecting with nature in pregnancy to looking back on a lifetime of experiencing wildlife, the reoccurring sentiment from almost every writer was that everyone fell in love with nature when they were young; and for the lucky ones among us, that love remains eternal.

In a time of pandemic, where a diet of life and death has been fed to us constantly through unnerving news reports and daily death tolls; many used the opportunity to reflect on nature the saviour, and its dutiful presence throughout the twists and turns of human life.

Although not Wildlife Bloggers themselves, two of the most personally important and interesting pieces I collected for the anthology came from my mother and grandmother (Rosemary Snowdon and Dorothy Knights). As the book is dedicated to my own children, and life stages and even mortality seem to be the order of the day, I used the opportunity to represent four generations of female wildlife lovers within my family.

Having found myself needing an emergency hysterectomy slap bang in the middle of this project, this was also my way of reaching out to the line of genetically connected women that I proudly stand among; sharing our stories and likenesses in a connected space, bound in paper – an ink and pulp iteration of a family tree, if you will.

My grandmother, currently in her 100th year, could neither type nor handwrite her entry. Although her memory continues to astound me, a combination of an unsteady hand, arthritis in her fingers and diminishing eyesight meant I would need to take a different approach. Dorothy's entry was formed through a series of interviews recorded and transcribed. Ever the journalist, I had interviewed my nan for fun back in 2008 to test out my new dictaphone in the days before smartphones could do it all – and even these recordings were dug up to the surface and various audio accounts woven into her book entry.

All in all, putting this book together has been the most satisfying and soulful of experiences – and who knows, if we sell enough copies*, perhaps I'll get to book those flights to Costa Rica after all?!

*The first £100 raised from sales of Connections with Nature *will be used to purchase 1 acre of rainforest land via the World Land Trust – similar to that which I would have visited in Peru. I haven't calculated exactly what it would take to make this book publishing venture carbon-neutral, but I think protecting an acre of rainforest is a good place to start!*

About The Wildlife Blogger Crowd

The Wildlife Blogger Crowd was founded by Kate Stephenson. Kate is a journalist, blogger and wildlife campaigner, as well as the creator of the successful nature and wildlife blog *Kate on Conservation*.

Kate has worked as Education Editor for *National Geographic Kids* magazine and Sub Editor for *Discovery Education*. She has written and edited for national and international media organisations, such as Discovery Communications, BBC and Channel 4. She is a trustee of international wildlife charity Born Free Foundation, and an ambassador for Ocean Conservation Trust and International Aid for the Protection and Welfare of Animals (IAPWA).

To mark the 10th anniversary of her *Kate on Conservation* blog, Kate founded The Wildlife Blogger Crowd; a collective of wildlife and eco-content creators spanning online bloggers, social media curators, podcasters, filmmakers and more.

The Wildlife Blogger Crowd is a diverse community of storytellers from across the globe, working together to amplify one another's voices in sharing a common passion for wildlife, nature and conservation – and communicating a desperate need to save. To find out more, or to join the crowd, head to: wildlifebloggercrowd.com

FOREWORD

Jonathan Scott

Nature is sacred, the source of all life; without it we would cease to exist in body and soul. Our connection to Nature is so important that there is a name for it – *biophilia* – meaning an affinity or love for Nature. Today, with more than 50% of people living in urban settings, many people have become disconnected from the natural world, believing that our survival depends on us rather than Nature. By 2050 it is estimated this number will have increased to 66%. For all of our astounding technology, our ability to invent and create, none of it would be possible without Nature and the inorganic world that together make up our exquisitely beautiful planet.

We have been fortunate to spend much of our time in the company of large charismatic animals at home in Kenya, not least the big cats of the Maasai Mara National Reserve such as the Marsh Pride of lions that we first started watching in 1977. Our connection to Nature feels all the more real from witnessing life and death on an almost daily basis; the eternal struggle between predator and prey to sustain themselves. Nature provides all of us with the ingredients of life – air, water, food, shelter – along with the joy of birdsong and breathtaking landscapes: the savannas, forests, deserts, mountains, oceans, rivers and polar regions that define our world and dazzle the eye with their beauty. These varied and complex ecosystems are home to millions of species, some so small that we do not even know they are there or even acknowledge their importance, along with the mighty elephants and giraffes that have trod these ancient landscapes for millennia, creations of nature's ingenuity, finished and complete in the web of life.

For Angela, an encounter in Tonga with a mother humpback whale and its calf, the eerie silence of the deep blue broken only by their exhalation as they surfaced beside her in an explosion of bubbles, is a never-to-be-forgotten moment. While for me, time spent with my first wild leopard in the 1970s and early 80s – a female I called Chui (meaning leopard in Swahili) and her cubs Light and Dark – allowed me to explore what it meant to be a leopard, the most elusive, enigmatic and adaptable of all big cats. I savoured every moment in her company as I gradually came to know her as a unique individual, learning to think like a leopard and predict where I might find her the following morning. The same is true of spending months at a time with the Marsh lions, becoming part of the pride while always respecting each one of them as "other" – not pets, not our friends, but creatures living out their own destiny unfettered by human values or judgements.

By encouraging people of all ages to share their love of the natural world with her own unique brand of energy and enthusiasm, ingenuity and creativity, Kate is playing a valuable part in reconnecting people to the wonder and joy that all of us can find in Nature. We just have to open our eyes and begin the adventure.

Jonathan and Angela Scott
The Big Cat People
www.bigcatpeople.com

PART ONE
IN THE BEGINNING

1

THE BIRDS
AND THE BABY

Kate Stephenson

The water trembles at the wriggle of my toes, sending a gentle ripple trundling outwards from the edge of my foot until it touches the invisible corners of the infinity pool and makes its escape by spilling over the edge.

A slosh, as the water hits the hidden overflow channel and I look up from where I'm seated to see an Antillean Crested Hummingbird flit by and hover for a second at a bright pink flower, purposefully extracting its irresistible nectar.

Breathe in. The Saint Lucia rainforest air drifts up from the trees below and fills my lungs with a new freshness. Exhale; and with it some of the heaviness of pregnancy seems to leave my swollen, aching body.

Birdwatching has become my solace as the weeks expand into months and the months turn into trimesters. At this stage I'm told I should be 'glowing', but before touching down and embracing the vibrant Caribbean island of Saint Lucia, I feel nothing but tormented.

I have lost count of the number of times my sleepless nights have been shrugged off as "nothing compared to what will come soon!", and as medical appointments have bled into medical appointments – all with the predictable diagnosis of "pregnancy: this is what you should expect for the next few months, and at least a few months following" – I've begun to accept that I'm slipping into a state of depression.

Carrying a child should be blissful, beautiful, 'earthy'. But the black dog walks beside me frequently and I can see him stand over me sometimes in sleep-deprived hallucinations. Saint Lucia's bird life seems to be gradually chirping, twittering and pecking him away. Of the 157 bird species that live on the island, it's the national bird, the Saint Lucia Parrot (*Amazona versicolor*), that I long to see. The Saint Lucia Parrot is one of five native parrot species found in the Commonwealth country, and I make it my mission to spot at least one of them before my time here is up.

We have six days.

On day two I have a proper appetite for the first time in weeks. Pregnancy has wreaked havoc with my immune system, and my thyroid levels and red blood cell count have plummeted below the acceptable line. I haven't eaten meat for years now, but the local chef gives a convincing argument for Saint Lucians building an economy around sustainably fishing the invasive and ecologically damaging Lionfish. On his recommendation I sample this dish and try traditional Saint Lucian banana cake for dessert. My body thanks me. On day three I have the energy to swim in the sea, respectfully gliding over coral and tropical fish. I snorkel, I dive down and touch the sand at the bottom and I remember what it feels like to not be bound by this new weight on my body. By day four, I sleep. I dream. Real dreams of rainforests and tropical coral reefs and sighting a blue-coloured parrot.

By day five I've walked, I've climbed, I've hiked. I've seen banana plantations and sunset mists roll through towering gum trees and encase fiddlehead ferns…but I haven't seen a parrot.

On my final day, I journey skyward through the Babonneau rainforest in a green gondola that gently rocks and climbs its way over

76 square kilometres of lush, protected rainforest. The island's aerial tram showcases the tropical rainforest, which is home to large wild boar; the unusual agouti; rodents; lizards and four different species of snake. I'm glad that the tram ride gives rest to my now fat, swollen feet.

At 430 metres above sea level we emerge from the treetops and are treated to incredible views of forest, clouds and distant ocean. We see hummingbirds; the Purple-Throated Carib and the Green-Throated Carib. We see magnolia shrubs and giant hibiscus flowers brought over from Jamaica. But I don't see a parrot. On the way back down, I realise it doesn't matter. I feel alive again. I feel like some of the fog in my mind has lifted. I feel like my baby and I are going to be just fine.

Drifting in and out of exhausted slumber as the taxi bumps and bounces its way towards the airport, our driver slows to a near halt. "Look!" he exclaims, pointing excitedly, "over there you can see our national bird; the parrot!"

My heart races as I bolt upwards in my seat and reach the taxicab window just in time to catch the slightest glimpse of colour pulling itself forwards through the humid afternoon air. I recognise the creature's methodic figure-eight wing movements.

At check-in a representative from Travel Saint Lucia hands me a blue linen bag with a smile; "For the baby," she adds. I open it to find a cuddly toy parrot.

Kate Stephenson is a writer and blogger. For 10 years she has run the wildlife blog *Kate on Conservation*. She has worked for numerous media organisations specialising in children's education, such as *National Geographic Kids*, *Discovery Education*, *Channel 4 Learning*, *Channel 4 Talent*, *BBC Blast* and *BBC Norfolk*. She is a

trustee of Born Free Foundation and founder of The Wildlife Blogger Crowd; a collective of wildlife and eco-content creators, spanning online bloggers, social media curators, podcasters, film-makers and more.

2

ONE SMALL STEP

Tiffany Francis-Baker

One night, last summer, in the last few weeks of pregnancy, I stepped out into the garden and met the gaze of a full moon, white and round, pouring down onto the Earth. To stumble upon a full moon when you're not expecting it is one of nature's greatest tricks – the shock that something not powered by electricity can be so bright – but something in that milky light calls out to our wilder selves.

The Moon is both friend and stranger, lingering on the edge of my life since I could first see out of my bedroom window, when my curtains were decorated with pastel elephants and balloons. I remember hearing stories about The Man on the Moon, and learning that somehow, a few years ago, we had flown there in a rocket and planted a flag. And yet, this bright ball in the sky is unreachable for me, unless Elon Musk invites me on one of his cosmic joyrides. It's unlikely I will ever walk on the Moon – but who knows? My great-grandchildren might.

In October 2020, NASA announced that, for the first time ever, scientists had identified water on the sunny side of the Moon. They also found the Moon's water sources were more widespread than previously thought, with pockets of ice hiding in some of its darker, more shadowy regions. This has excited the scientific community because water is such an essential resource for space exploration, and if water can be extracted from the Moon, it means space shuttles can carry less water and make room for more equipment. It also means that we can more easily return astronauts to the Moon, and create long-term habitats on the lunar surface to use as a base for exploring Mars.

What does this mean for the future of the human race? The film-maker Dr Nelly Ben Hayoun has been exploring ideas around a lunar diaspora and the language we use to talk about the Moon. As a daughter of immigrants, she warns that humans could be set to repeat the same mistakes of colonialism, empire and war; noting how space agencies and private investors are already turning the Moon into a place where resources will be exploited, particularly through mining. 'I can't believe,' she says, 'that as a human species we can't come up with fresh thinking and new ways to apprehend politics, nation states and economics. It is urgent that we focus on rethinking these plans now before others define the future of humanity on our behalf without any ethical, historical or creative considerations.'

When I was five years old, I visited the Kennedy Space Center in Florida on a family holiday. It was from there that half a century ago, the Apollo 11 spacecraft launched and landed two men on the Moon. During our visit we watched a space shuttle launch into a blue sky. I still have the ticket in a drawer somewhere, and a photo of me before lift-off, honey-blonde curls in a tangle and a look of wonder at what I was about to see. Perhaps this was the first time I realised how precious and fragile our own planet is – how much life exists on this tiny orb.

When the Voyager 1 space probe took the famous *Pale Blue Dot* photograph in 1990, we saw our planet for what it really was: a single pixel against the vastness of outer space. It is strange that we have become so determined to explore new worlds when we can't even look after the one we have. How many billions do we spend on space travel, when all the technology and resources are available to stop climate chaos, if governments would only work together and commit to footing the bill?

Certain groups of humans have a history of colonising places they have never been, drawing maps and marking boundaries, assuming they have a right to something just because they have the willpower, or a religious belief, or simply the most powerful technology. In 1923, the English mountaineer George Mallory was asked by a *New York Times* reporter why he wanted to climb Mount Everest. 'Because it's there,' he replied. 'Its existence is a challenge. The answer is instinctive, a part, I suppose, of man's desire to conquer the universe.' But is it inevitable for us to want to 'conquer the universe'? I wonder whether we accept these ideas as truth because it's easier than trying to change our collective mindset. There are plenty of examples of human communities living in a more harmonious, symbiotic relationship with nature, who don't assume the world is laid out for them on a plate, to gorge on and gather up in their fists. But I am just as much to blame. I accept our capitalist society, buy cheap food and the occasional cheap jumper. And I would jump at the chance to visit the Moon – because it's there.

'One Small Step' is an extract from the book Woodland Essays: Volume One/Silver Birch, *available to buy at: tiffanyfrancisbaker.com/shop*

Tiffany Francis-Baker is a nature writer, illustrator, mother and small-business owner from the South Downs in Hampshire. She makes stationery and gifts inspired by the natural world, all ethically sourced and designed to last. She is also the author of six books, including *Dark Skies: A Journey into the Wild Night*. In 2019 she was a writer-in-residence for Forestry England, and

she has written for the *Guardian*, *Harper's Bazaar*, *BBC Wildlife*, *BBC Countryfile* and *Resurgence & Ecologist*. Find out more at: tiffanyfrancisbaker.com

3

A FRESH APPROACH

Joe Harkness

A derisory laugh, pumping – almost rattling – sounds out behind us. They call it a 'yaffle' and it's difficult to find a different word to capture the sound. *'Did you hear that?'* I ask her, knowing that she isn't going to reply. *'That's a Green Woodpecker.'* Suddenly, as if it heard me, an almost luminous-green bird comes bounding over our heads and along the tree-lined path. Its bright red cap gives it an almost clown-like appearance, quite apt then for its chuckling call. I turn so that she can see from within the sling and point it out as it undulates away from us in flight.

It seems that with every step we take, a 'new' Skylark gives flight. A bubbling and almost-constant backing track of nostalgic melody surrounds us. *'Can you hear the Skylarks?'* I ask her, already knowing the answer. A pair of Dunnocks flick across from the fence line and onto the gorse, quickly disappearing into prickly growth. I know she can smell the gorse and so I tell her about it, *'That smell is gorse, it smells like coconut, you've tried coconut!'*

You see, it's not about me and my own experience of being outside anymore. She's the number one priority and I want to share it all with her, not force it upon her. I just want to talk to her about what she can see, hear and smell (she's not tasting much as she keeps chewing on the shoulder strap of the sling). Occasionally, she acknowledges me or our surroundings, screeching at a dog walker or turning to look towards wherever I'm pointing. It's a constant and calming conversation, albeit particularly one-sided. We turn to walk along the southerly path, back to where we began our walk.

On this side, the wind is too strong for her and I have to put her hood up and, eventually, the wind-protector on the sling. There's no focus on being immersed outside anymore, just on getting her back to the car. Bird moments become briefer. The onomatopoeic chant of a Chiffchaff beats over from the car park, I tell her all about it, its journey and how it signals spring. How Daddy has written about them in his book and that this season is a time of wonder and new emergence.

We're almost back to our starting point and the buffering has stopped, for there's more shelter in the south-eastern corner of the reversion field. The cover and hood come down and we stop to look at the horses in the paddock. A scratchy subsong emerges from the hedge that borders the horse fields; and it blossoms into a fruitful fluted melody – a Blackcap. She laughs at the horses, they always make her laugh. I smile at the Blackcap song and the reassurance it brings.

As we hop the fence to the track where the car is parked, a lone Fieldfare sits atop the outpost tree down the track. It should be moving on now, as we are, and I like the comparison. It's on the tree that has been the staging post for many a Ring Ouzel and the singing spot for many a Mistle Thrush. I inform her about the significance of the tree and she shrieks in delight, but at the horses again, not the reminiscence. Off it flies to continue onward, as we do, to the car and then home.

A yew full of Thrushes

People say *"keep walking"* and *"walk it off"* which in principle, is a lovely idea. Except, when the pain is an all-day occurrence and feels like a tooth root being tweaked by a dentist, in your leg, permanently; it can be hard to listen to any sound advice. She doesn't know about the pain. Daddy wincing when he moves is funny – he is playing a game. That recognisable feeling of cabin fever has started to creep up again and the earlier suggestion to go for a walk seems ever-wiser. Back clicking, face grimacing and leg semi-buckling; it is time to get ready. Mummy calls through, requesting two carrots and a parsnip from the farm shop if we are going that way. We have a mission.

Toddler mittens. Why is it such a fiddle to put them on? Puddle suit... no, she can wrap up in the cosy-toes pram cover, like a fleecy sleeping bag for a pushchair. The pink woolly hat with the white bobble on top is non-negotiable though. She usually pulls it off, but seems to welcome its warmth in the cold porch, as if she is pre-empting the first days of meteorological winter unfurling outside the door. We are both wrapped up for our morning stroll and both happily anticipating some fresh, chill air.

The ancient trader's lane bisects the southern end of the town boundary and runs along the edge of a smallholding. *"Neigh neighs?"* she asks. Later, we will walk back past the horses. She points to the ageing brickwork of the walled alleyway, reaching out to run her hands along its crumbling red and black bricks; tracing their history. We push past a wooden door, set in the wall and as tradition of this path walk tells, she has to *"knock knock"* on it, even though no-one ever answers. Through the black bike bars at the end, under the brick arch, we head towards the churchyard.

The yews lining the path are foreboding. We watched a BBC news short on the folklore of yews a few weeks before. Their poison: fatal; their connotations with death: poignant. They are beautiful trees though, with deep hewn scaling on their trunks and bright, blood-red berries, warning of danger but equally as alluring. In the churchyard they are also a haven for our local avifauna, acting as a central focus in the brick-filled market square. As we pass under, several birds dart between the trees and she proclaims *"bur-ee"* at their sudden appearance.

We stop for a moment. Two Mistle Thrushes are atop the church tower and we crane our heads, giddily, to see them. One flies down into the right-hand yew, where it joins up with two Song Thrushes who are sitting out, framed within small cavernous openings between the higher branches. They softly *tick* to each other as the Mistle Thrushes *rattle* back and forth. Blackbirds *chup* away tenderly. It's a soothing sonic chorus of gentle bird calls – fitting for the place of reflection we are walking through. As we walk away, the subtle *tseep* of two departing Redwing passes over us in farewell. We leave behind the yew full of thrushes.

Nap-time, a sodden pushchair and over 1,000 Starlings

You can tell when she is tired. She starts to suck her thumb more vigorously and strokes her earlobe, plus her eyelids look noticeably heavy. She has been tired for half an hour now, in fact, she is overtired and fighting her body's natural urge to sleep. Every time she is laid down on the sofa and wrapped up, she looks like she is about to succumb, then smiles and starts to stroke my face – I cannot help but smile back – then it becomes a game. It is probably because she fell asleep in the car seat on the way back from the food shopping. Yes! The car seat! She has never been driven to sleep purposely, but if she misses this nap then the repercussions could continue into the ensuing days. We are going to give it a try.

Within five minutes of being in the seat, she is asleep and we are driving without purpose. The off-road buggy, rain cover and changing bag are all in the car boot, so really, we can drive anywhere. She needs to sleep for an hour, ideally, so we head away from town and, suddenly, the coast seems like the perfect destination, where we can get out and go for a walk. It starts to rain, not that heavily, but it is persistent and the wipers have to be clicked up into second gear to clear away the raindrops. The sky is much greyer when we reach the cricket club car park and as we've only been driving for forty minutes, the engine will have to keep running to continue the sensation that we are still on the move.

Five clicks of the handbrake and she is awake, grizzling for a snack and some water. The buggy is put up, she is hastily but gently put in it, the canopy is over, rain cover on and we are off up the old coastwatch track in the driving rain. The buggy's rough tread helps it to negotiate the muddy brown puddles and we talk all the way to the squat brick shelter. To be fair, though, it's a one-sided conversation about the importance of good sleep patterns and the wonder of bird migration. The rain's tenacity increases and it bounces off the rain cover, splashing into the canvas bag tray at the bottom. She's happy, babbling and laughing each time that the buggy stops and I crouch down to look through her 'viewing hatch'. We smile and continue walking.

The elder bush is alive with the movement of birds. We can see several Chaffinches, some Reed Buntings and a charm of Goldfinches – that all take flight, coalesce and then separate into the surrounding bushes. We make it to the shelter and as we enter, a Goldcrest sits sodden on the brick windowsill (albeit, long devoid of an actual window), visibly exhausted and trembling. It does not show concern for our presence and stays for a few minutes watching, as she eats some coconut rolls and has some water; the Goldcrest, drying.

We talk about the journey these birds will have just undertaken; the weather, the loneliness – the magic! The Starlings start to trickle over the cliff like a black band twanging in the wind. They stay in formation, ordered and purposeful, as they continue to stream over the clifftop.

Over the next ten minutes or so, hundreds of them emerge from the misty murk and arrow into the beet tops of the field next to the shelter. She has seen the miracle that is bird migration first-hand. I smile – she giggles – and we begin to walk back down the track, once again negotiating the pockmarks and puddles.

Joe Harkness is the author of the book *Bird Therapy*. He writes and speaks about the benefits of birdwatching for mental health and well-being. As well as living with various issues himself, he works in special education and is highly experienced at connecting with vulnerable people. Joe has also written for numerous publications, including: *The Guardian, Condé Nast Traveller, BBC Wildlife Magazine, inews, Birdwatch Magazine* and *Birdwatching Magazine*.

4

THE SECRET GARDEN AND WHAT ONCE WAS

Rosemary Snowdon

Sensory overload; that's the way I remember experiencing nature in my early childhood. Those memories ingrained in my senses mean that nowadays, a smell, or a sound, or something that I see, can transport my mind instantly back to my childhood days.

I have vivid memories of spending time in a family with no car and little money, enjoying many wonderful wildlife experiences. We walked long distances; my mum, my dad, my brother and I, but we never seemed to get tired or even notice how far we had walked or how much further we had to go.

We lived in the small market town of Thetford in Norfolk, surrounded by fields and woodland.

The town was originally set up as a trading place at the intersection of two rivers: the River Little Ouse and the River Thet. The combination of all these habitats provided an abundance of biodiversity.

Living here meant that my family and I regularly had the chance to see a variety of wildlife such as Muntjac and Roe Deer, Woodpeckers, Kingfisher, Heron and numerous other birds. Every time we walked the hour-long round trip to the town's high street, or journeyed further afield, it felt like an adventure – as we never quite knew what we might encounter along the way. When I was young, my father used to tease me and say, "We might see a giraffe or an elephant" – and for a long time I kept looking and hoping!

Each week my dad would take us to the place where he grew up, a small cluster of cottages in a village called Kilverstone, to visit the graves of his father and his younger brother: a childhood victim of rheumatic fever. My father, who as a 12-year-old tangled with the same deadly disease that would claim his 10-year-old brother's life, was a walking ode to the fragility of life on earth – even to my childhood self.

To reach these quiet final resting places, which were often strewn with berries plucked by birds from the nearby holly bushes or the two impressive rowan trees which stood nearby, we had to walk to the outskirts of the town, crossing over a railway line and traipsing through an untouched lane enshrined by high hedges and tall trees. I remember how this felt like an adventure in itself, as the railway crossing was always unmanned with no barriers in place, and my brother and I used to hope we would see a train before running across the tracks.

Dad always had a box of Smarties in his pocket and would hand them out as we skipped along. Nearing the church graveyard, we had to pass a wonderful building that seemed huge and castle-like to my youthful mind's eye: Kilverstone Hall was owned by Lord and Lady Fisher.

Running alongside the impressive Hall was a flint wall, which seemed unnervingly tall to us as children. Much to my mother's disapproval, my father would allow us to teeter along the top of the wall to complete the last few yards of the journey. I have the most treasured memories of being high above ground, steadying myself on the wall to catch a glimpse into the magnificent gardens of this beautiful hall.

My brother and I learned to keep very quiet atop the wall, because doing so increased our chances of eyeing the spectacular sight of the resident Golden Pheasants in their bright oriental colours, and the blue and white Peacocks which would shake their enormous tails and call out across the lush green gardens. Their cries were eerie and loud, and often made me jump, so that I could hear my heart thumping. With the height of the wall never far from my mind, I would fancy myself a skilled tightrope walker, twisting and stretching to catch a glimpse of a displaying Peacock, or to spot the elusive lone white bird strutting around with a crown on its head.

The Golden Pheasants were so brightly coloured with such beautiful feathers and long tails, that I never wanted to move on or get down from the wall. I fell several times grazing my knees, after becoming so transfixed on the search for what I thought was the ultimate treasure you could find. My brother would laugh at me and say: "Look where you are going, twit!" and Mum would scold him. My dad would laugh and lift me back onto the wall.

Nowadays, I frequently pass the overgrown wall, which seems quite small now. On occasion, I haven't been able to resist the urge to stand on tiptoe and peak in at the neglected gardens, empty of the beautiful wildlife that once existed there. I find myself imagining the taste of my favourite Smarties, the stinging feel of grazed knees and the sound of my father's laughter. I catch myself listening for the Peacocks' shrill cries and searching for the bright feathers among the memories of lush foliage and well-kempt gardens; knowing they have long gone. Sadly, so has my beloved father, but the pleasure of nature, and of life itself that he passed on to me, always remains.

Rosemary Snowdon is a retired nursery school teacher. During her career, she was passionate about introducing children to the wonders of nature through venturing outside and exploring their local

environment – or using imaginative play to understand the workings of the natural world. Nowadays, she continues to realise that passion through the many hours spent with her seven grandchildren.

5

BETWEEN GIRL AND BIRD

Jenny Allan

Locked in a stiff-winged flight, it soars and it glides in the endless skies above the cliffs where the only law is gravity. Down it swoops, to eye height, mere metres from my being – a wild look in its eyes; eyes that have gazed over vast oceans in its nomadic life: a Fulmar.

A connection forms between girl and bird, invisible tendrils; a connection: one indescribable but noticeable, and one that can soothe every turmoil in the brain.

Back down to earth and Turnstones are running frantically, never stopping, eking out every nutrient in the algae, while Pied Wagtails leisurely hop from seaweed pile to seaweed pile.

A shadow overhead interrupts my staring, and wandering thoughts, a Great Black-Backed Gull, the largest gull on Earth! Its wings and back a shade of grey only just lighter than black, and (despite its size) a bird that seems to have more grace than its cousin the Herring Gull.

Over the writhing seas it flies, out of sight into the next bay along, attracting my eyes offshore and to a stream of black shapes: Cormorants. Upwards of a hundred of them, their flock morphing and changing with every passing second, the seas equivalent to a Starling murmuration – simple but eye-catching.

Through the familiar and comforting white noise of the crashing waves I hear a sound, mournful and haunting, the cry of the beach and wilds of the coast, a Curlew. Low and fast it flies, then lands on a rock, it stands tall and proud, proclaiming this to be its rightful home.

On I walk, sand subsiding underfoot with every step I take. Feral Pigeons roost on chalk ledges on the looming cliffs, each bird's plumage a different pattern of colour palettes. At the top of these looming cliffs are bushes, their roots clinging for dear life to the unforgiving chalk, Sparrows chirp loudly from here, announcing their presence to all who will listen.

Further along and I find Starlings, in dart-like flocks, the sun behind them, bleaching out their iridescence to plain black.

I climb steps embedded in the rising cliff, and the faint 't-seep' of a Redwing heralds the end of my walk. My beach walk serves as, a wild front in an urban area, an untamed place in a tamed world.

Returning to the tamed world will not sever the bond that nature has created; it will always be there, through every day and night, through every maelstrom in the mind and through every wild space, and urban place. I am part of nature, we all are, no matter how much the modern world tries to hide this, those tendrils of connection will never falter.

Jenny Allan is a young naturalist interested in all wildlife from birds to bats, to moths and springtails. She also a keen wildlife photography and a trainee bird ringer, often found roaming her local beaches and green spaces in search for wild places and the wildlife that lives there. Find out more at: theyoungnaturenerd. wordpress.com

6

THE WILD IN ALL OF US

Tania Roa

"Wild child" is what they used to call my brother. I remember being so jealous of that title. "But I want to be the wild one," I would think to myself. I was the one who leaped at the opportunity to hold a snake. I was the first one to jump off that raft when we were cruising down that Colombian river. "I'm the real wild one," I would often tell myself. Looking back, I don't think I was upset that I didn't have my brother's nickname. I think I was upset that no-one seemed to see what I saw.

The way feathery, slimy, and scaly creatures moved. The formations I would find in clouds and stars. The way water moved so effortlessly, yet so abruptly, through rock formations and over tree roots. I found everything about nature and wildlife so fascinating. I still look over mountainous landscapes and feel overwhelmed with joy. I still swim in the ocean and find peace, grace, and excitement. The admiration I have felt for nature has never ceased. If anything, it has only grown fonder.

After more than 20 years of walking on this Earth, I continue to find new ways to observe how nature works. Through photography, I can catch glimpses of animals going about their day. I can zoom in and examine the details of their various colours. After some time, I began noticing what types of trees certain birds enjoy. I rediscovered the local California beaches with only a pair of goggles. I now identify the ant trails in my backyard, and I make sure to step over them.

Photography has, literally and figuratively, provided me with a new lens. I now see the world differently. I am captivated by the details of each animal rather than being focused on what species they are. I notice their quirks and personalities. I recognise when a wild animal does not find my presence comforting or when it curiously investigates me and my camera. I see them for *who* they are, not merely *what* they are.

Each wildlife encounter is memorable, I walk away in awe every time. There is something about seeing species interacting with the Earth that reminds me of how similar they are to us, and indeed how similar we are to them. It is a constant reminder of how this beautiful blue-green planet is one great big home, and because of that, there is nothing that can disconnect me from those wild animals.

The fact is, we all have nature inside of us. She runs through our veins, our bones, and into our soul. She never leaves our side because attempting to separate a person from nature is like trying to separate yourself from your spirit. It is impossible.

Sure, you can try to take humans out of nature. You can build asphalt roads, sky-high buildings, and telephone poles. You can create millions of gadgets, toys, and other material goods. You can even take away the remaining plants and trees breaking their way through the cement. But even after all of that, we humans continue longing for more. A void remains – one that refuses to fill up with the latest trend. Sometimes we do not realise where this void comes from until we become gravely sick. Once our neighbours suffer from asthma, or our eyes grow tired of looking at screens, or until our minds forget the feeling of grass in our toes, we have an epiphany.

We look around at our stale environment, and we finally understand what is missing. Then, in the end, all those efforts to build a divide between humans and nature are defeated. Sure, you can try to take humans out of nature, but it does not take them long to find their way back.

Mother Earth stays with us wherever we go, and for that, I am grateful.

Tania Roa resides in Southern California, where she works at a climate and environmental non-profit. She has a Master of Science in Animals and Public Policy and a passion for all things nature and wildlife. As well as advocating for wild animals, she enjoys studying the connections between people's well-being, animal welfare, and the health of our planet. Tania regularly posts about climate and environmental justice on her social media platforms.

7

THE BARN OWL FEATHER

Benjamin Fallow and Michelle Fossey

'It's a Barn Owl feather! It's my nature treasure for the day!' It was a small flight feather, in perfect condition.

'Can you hear it?' Benji flapped it up and down past my ear.

'That's how you tell if it's an owl's feather, 'cause they're silent in flight, such an incredible find!'

'People used to be scared of Barn Owls because they fly completely silently, and have such a piercing screech! But I think they bring good luck, they're so beautiful and their hearing is incredible!' Benji was explaining it all to me on our walk by the Barn Owl tree.

'The shape of their face reflects sound to their ear openings! The Barn Owl's left ear is higher up on its head than its right ear. The medulla is the bit of their brain that understands hearing, it's the biggest of any creature, and that's why they are able to hear so well!'

Every time we pass this tree Benji searches the ground hoping for a feather. He found this Barn Owl feather in the first lockdown, and drew it from real life.

Seven-year-old Benjamin Fallow is a young artist and naturalist. He loves learning everything he can about animals, insects and plants, and he's passionate about protecting nature and wildlife. Benji draws and paints from nature – he's been carrying paper and pens in his backpack since he was three.

During lockdown, Benji won a national nature-writing competition for his age group, *Nature on your Doorstep* with Lucy McRobert, and was featured on Chris Packham's *Self-Isolating Bird Club*. His story was published in *BBC Wildlife*.

Benji started sharing his artwork on Instagram during lockdown, and was amazed when he was featured on Chris Packham's show with his nature artwork too! He's been featured on Instagram by the Wildlife Trusts and the Natural History Museum, and on Twitter by the RSPB. Sharing his artwork he's received amazing encouragement from Sir David Attenborough and many of his favourite nature artists. Benji wants to use his artwork to encourage people to care for nature. Michelle is Benji's mum.

The Barn Owl Feather by Benjamin Fallow

8
PASSING ON A PASSION

Rachael Barber

My son, Toby, smiles at a Brambling *(left)*. He is only just beginning his wildlife adventures and still his little face creases up into a huge smile whenever he sees a bird.

My daughter, Robyn, releases a Kingfisher *(below)*. I love seeing her delight at holding a bird; her knowledge of wildlife at such a young age astounds me.

RACHAEL BARBER

← *The Barn Owl Feather* cont.

Opposite page, clockwise from top left:
The Barn Owl Feather by Benjamin Fallow. Age 6. Pencil on paper, 27 May 2020. The feather is about 12cm long and Benji's drawing is life-size.

Barn Owl by Benjamin Fallow. Age 6. Pencil on paper, 2 July 2020.

Benji uses his feather to try to get the details on his barn owl painting just right.

Benji holds a barn owl feather.

RACHAEL BARBER

29

9
GRASPING FOR EDEN
Lize Gibson-Hall

Lize Gibson-Hall

10
SWAN SALUTATION
Steve Shand

Steve Shand

11
JUVENILE PEREGRINES

Barry Madden

12
A DOG'S PERSPECTIVE

Charlotte Ditchburn

13
MOORLAND FAIRGROUND

Alicia Hayden

The Day of the Hare by Rebecca Gibson

14

THE DAY OF THE HARE

Rebecca Gibson

When the alarm sounded at 4:30am, I almost sunk straight back to sleep. But for the past few mornings, when I'd woken at a more civilised time, gorgeous 'golden hour' light had been shimmering through the curtains and I'd regretted not being a part of it. So, I shovelled down some breakfast cereal and faced the darkness.

I knew there were hares nearby as I often saw them dashing across open fields, too fast and far away for a photo. Like most wildlife they like their early mornings, so I raced the sun and arrived at first light. If I parked up and sat still, windows down safari style, I thought maybe they might appear a bit closer.

Cars can be excellent wildlife hides. Foraging pheasants kept me company while I waited, either unaware or unfazed by me. Every now and then a male flapped his wings and screeched at the sky, making me jump. In the otherwise silent field he was deafening.

I'd positioned myself so I could look down a narrow farm track and my chest tightened when a hare hopped across it. Hares are masters of trickery. They pad along without a sound and vanish when they stand still.

By 9am my hands were numb. The pheasants were still scratching around and I tried to photograph the exact moment the male decided to call, but he was too preoccupied with feeding to look up. I was just about to put my camera back down when my gaze drifted behind him to a hare crouched beside a hay bale.

I froze, actually hearing my heart thud as it padded towards me. Even though it could see me, there was something about the car hide that had relaxed it enough to check me out. Once it was ten feet from my lens, the hare sat and stared right at me. We were so close I had to somehow zoom out without moving. Moments later, the hare turned and lolloped back behind the bale.

Once I was sure it had gone I checked the photos, convinced I'd chopped its ears off frame in my haste to zoom out. But I'd got the shot, and for the first time in eleven years of photography I cried looking at my camera screen. The combination of shock, joy and relief was overwhelming and I almost couldn't believe what had happened.

I don't think there's anything more special than when wildlife chooses to interact with you. Chasing a wild animal is never the answer – you won't get the photo you want and, far more importantly, you'll disturb it. Sitting silent and still in my car was the best thing I could have done. The hare decided to approach me, not the other way round, and the result was a brief but beautifully intimate connection between us.

The 4:30am alarm was a distant memory.

Rebecca Gibson is a wildlife writer, who loves encouraging people to connect with nature and discover the wonders of British wildlife. She created the blog *Rebecca One Wing* in 2015 to document her travels and wild discoveries around the UK, using photography and art as visual accompaniments to her writing. Since moving to Scotland, she has blogged with a particular focus on coastal and marine species with an emphasis on birds and mammals. Find out more at: rebeccaonthewing.com/blog

PART TWO
EVOLVING PERSPECTIVES

15

FLEETING YOUTH

Dorothy Knights

The early years of my childhood were spent in the Norfolk countryside, cycling from my hometown of Thetford to nearby Kilverstone, Swaffham and Brandon. Those were simpler times, back in the 1920s and '30s. My best friends were my neighbours – back then you were born in your mother's home – so my friends, my sister and I, were all born on the same street.

As children we climbed and played on the Charles Burrell traction engines; huge great machines that had wheels much taller than I was. These great vehicles were a sight to behold when we were so used to seeing horses walking on grass pathways. It would be some time before we ever saw a motor car.

Summer days were spent scrumping for apples in the grounds of a large hall that belonged to the Kilverstone Estate – until we were chased away for trespassing by PC Bell; Ding-a-bell as we all called him. Dinga, who was a notorious spoilsport to all those of our own age, was in fact a cousin of mine; in the days of small towns and large families, I had a good many cousins living nearby.

Things were simple and straightforward then; everybody knew everybody and it never really occurred to us that there was a world outside of the life we were living. We had everything we needed on our doorstep, and anything we didn't have, we didn't need.

I would go on to marry the boy who lived on the edge of Kilverstone Estate, our favourite apple-scrumping spot, and we went on to have four children together – two boys and two girls – the first of each were born during the years my husband was away. The second were my husband's chance to be involved with his children while they were young; having lost his first four years of fatherhood to being Tail-End-Charlie, sitting in the cramped and freezing cold conditions of the rear gunner's spot in a Lancaster bomber. Hurtling through the sky backwards was how he spent the entire war – apart from when his plane was shot down and he was hidden up by the Dutch resistance – and then a posting in Italy immediately following the war. He eventually got home in 1947.

When the war came, I had to leave the Norfolk countryside behind for the first time in my life; at 17 years old, I was old enough to join the war effort. My best friend Joan and I, being of the same age and from the same street, were both taken by our fathers to the local train station when we were called up together in September 1941. In all the commotion we stood and watched as our dads loaded our beloved bicycles onto the train for us.

We were all given tickets that told you where you would be going. I was given a different colour from Joan's, which meant we would be stationed in different places, doing different things. I kept looking and looking for another yellow ticket like mine – yellow meant electrical engineering.

It seemed a long time before Mildred and I found each other with our matching tickets, but we stayed together for the whole of the war after that. We started the first 11 weeks at a Government Training Centre in Letchworth Garden City. Although a Garden City was supposed to preserve the countryside, these places didn't look much like the countryside to me. After the Government Training Centre we were sent to our digs in Welwyn Garden City – which wasn't much like the countryside either. Though it was certainly beautiful with its straight rows of blossoming trees.

For a while we stayed with Mrs Brown; Ma Brown as we all called her. She was a great big lady – both myself and Mildred were afraid of her. She turned out to be a lovely person, but it took a while for us to warm up to her; and likewise it took her a while to warm up to us. A lot of people had a thing about us young countryfolk at that time, but the war would soon change all that.

Our work days would start at 4am, and that was after we'd walked the hour it took to get to the De Havilland engineering factory in Hatfield from our digs in Welwyn Garden City. We were still only 17 at the time – there were seven of us girls, and five prisoners of war doing the work that we did at those grinding machines.

One Friday afternoon, we arrived home from a long day in the factory to find Ma Brown stood out on the pavement with a wheelbarrow; "Right you girls, if you want a warm by the fire tonight you better get up in those woods and do a bit of sticking," she announced. In other words, we had to go to the woods and find some sticks that were good enough to go on the fire, before we could have the chance to rest and warm up.

Having grown up in the country though, this kind of work was at least a lot more familiar than the clinking of metal and the hum of giant machinery that I'd come to spend my days around. Fetching kindling from the woods was a small glimpse into the life I'd left behind.

But life, I have learnt, will always move and change. I came to admire Ma Brown, and made lifelong friends during those years in the factory; where I would spend my 21st birthday. I grew to love Hertfordshire too, cycling all round Welwyn Garden City, Hatfield, St Albans, Borehamwood, and we even using our rare moments of spare time to explore all the free museums in London between the bomb raids – so many things I didn't know I had to learn.

The war forced us to change perspectives on life. Moments were fleeting – even my wedding reception was interrupted when my husband and all our guests, who were his flight squadron, were called back to their base in Lakenheath and sent out to spend the night carrying out an air raid over Berlin. But that said, it was a good job he was in the RAF, because it meant I could have a wedding dress. We made mine out of a parachute he'd used to bail out with; which had ended up getting torn. Not too torn that we couldn't do anything with it as a dress though.

Like the changing of the seasons you must accept that life always changes too; sometimes for better, sometimes for worse. Like sometimes horses and grass roads get swapped for roads and motor cars; a parachute might save a life and still be put to good use as a wedding dress; and sometimes countryside becomes town, and cities get turned back into gardens.

Dorothy Knights is in her 100th year. Spending 100 years living on our planet has meant she has seen many changes, which has left her with the profound sense that she has lived long enough to know that there's a chance for everything to come back around.

16

SAVE THE HOUSE SPARROW

Harry Munt

People like exciting, flashy wildlife. It's a fact. And if you were to ask a set of conservationists what their dream job would be, many would likely cite ideals of working with some exciting, exotic species. Perhaps tracking big game in Africa or rejuvenating exotic reef systems.

Indeed, when you were young, you probably knew all about the Olympian creatures of the Serengeti, yet nothing about the little hidden wonders right on your doorstep.

This is because 'common' wildlife is now often disregarded. A riot of Feral Pigeons in a city centre are seemingly absorbed by the paving stones they waddle around on. Ceramic rooftops decorated with the puffy, pompous bodies of House Sparrows are so common they're invisible.

I'm guilty of this too. On my home turf, haunted by Kestrels, Kites, and dazzling rainforests of orchids, it may seem obvious what I go there searching for. The gangs of Magpie or kits of Wood Pigeon vanish into the scrub.

But surely, it should be the other way round? Our 'common' species are, after all, those that best understand the language of life and how best to adapt to it. It also turns out, that not all of these 'common' species are as common as perceived.

Take House Sparrows, for example. Often invisible, they might seem to plague some places, where their rapacious calls and iron-black bills could feel like the only birdlife around.

However, in Britain, these little cheerful treasures are disappearing. Between 1966 and 2019, nearly 50 were lost each hour. In London, over just one decade – 1996 to 2004 – their population fell by 60%, with national declines at over 70% since 1977.

When a species starts vanishing, there are usually two reactions: the first is simply nothing. People don't seem to take notice, and therefore nothing happens; for example, you probably remember when the first bluebell flowered in Spring, but how about the last?

The second, is when that species becomes widely recognised as rare, and therefore there is a higher value placed on spotting one; think about it – if you spotted a Curlew nest 50 years ago, would you have been more excited about it then, or does it feel more special today, after their population has nosedived by 65%?

Sadly, the story of the House Sparrow decline often aligns with the first of these reactions. Despite a quarter of gardens losing them in recent years, they're 'common', so why bother conserving them?

I was guilty of dismissing this charming species too, at first, until one particular summer spent in a petite little caravan in South Devon, right next to the largest Kittiwake colony in Britain. The sight was breathtaking. You'd be forgiven for thinking the colony was one beating organism, sliding off the cliffs and skimming the sea for food.

However, I was also amazed by the sheer number of birds living amongst the dense caravans themselves. Colossal Black-Backed Gulls soared on warm updrafts. Beady slate Jackdaws probed the lawns. Dunnocks skulked in the stomachs of bushes. And at the centre of this urban bird metropolis were the House Sparrows.

Beauty, it turns out, is genuinely within the eye of the beholder. While other birders might not even bother their notebooks with them, I could've spent hours with the House Sparrows. It was one special encounter with a brave-hearted male, who came to perch just less than a ruler's length from my face, and something about that cheeky glint in his eyes that made me fall in love with the little things.

Looking at a bird on the surface is clearly the wrong way to appreciate it. The House Sparrow is 'dull and common' at surface level, but beyond appearances, they're incredibly complex. They've made their homes everywhere from abandoned coal mines to dizzying heights on the Empire State Building and they're resourceful enough to make a meal out of everything from lizards to lettuce.

If you take the time to admire their finer details, you'll realise how visually stunning they are too. The males' tough, bulky beaks are more like pocket-sized black axes than bills; their mottled chestnut suits perfectly blend with almost any backdrop, while also communicating social rank to others; and most beautiful of all are those vibrant little eyes, like vibrant swirling galaxies.

When you look at a creature like the House Sparrow out of context, you see it from a completely different perspective. Take Pigeons: regularly dismissed as 'common, googly-eyed and stupid', but standing alone, they are beautifully complex creatures, that over billions of years of evolution have mastered the magical ability of flight! How many humans can do that?

Since observing House Sparrows more out of context, as opposed to beside Merlins or Kittiwakes, I've noticed how beautiful they are and in a unique way I feel a kind of connection with them.

When out in the garden, for example, there's almost a mutual understanding; an unspoken communication between us; a sort of interest, but respect, which you can have with any animal. It doesn't have to be big, flashy or majestic, just remember 'beauty is always in the eye of the beholder'.

Harry Munt is the founding member of Save the House Sparrows: a small group of like-minded people, working together to help stop the decline of the humble House Sparrow through education and good old hands-on conservation, such as installing bird boxes. You can find out more at: savethehousesparrow.com

17

THE OWLS NEXT DOOR

Jack Wright

Every January, birders up and down the country take part in the Big Garden Birdwatch and whilst tallying Sparrows passes the time easily enough, we long to see something exotic on the doorstep. A Red Kite swooping in or a Capercaillie popping round. We can all dream.

While you can only count the birds that you can literally see, if I were to have been extra cheeky, I could have recorded an exceptionally rare species, whose hidden presence was as unmistakeable as it was impressive. A bird that is widely idolised among wildlife lovers and members of the public alike; a bird of which the mere sighting causes instantaneous tantalisation. In a simple ash tree in my humble Norfolk garden, I had an active nest of Barn Owls. For at least three years, I was privileged enough to have a front row seat viewing the lives of these astonishing birds. This is the story of The Owls Next Door...

The ash tree in question faced the main road through my village and aside from a single small field, my house was surrounded by other bungalows and barns. As a child, I'd look at this giant tree with a round hole in the front and imagine that a wise old owl would live there, which, come to think of it, would actually transpire to be an amazing prediction.

To my knowledge, no Barn Owl or any other species lived in this tree cavity. Having lived there all my life, I'm sure I would have spotted something sooner, so for most of my life, the idea of anything calling that tree a home was a pipe dream.

One autumn afternoon in 2009, our neighbours rushed to our door and exclaimed that they'd seen a Barn Owl enter the tree. Cue unbridled excitement from little me. I'd known that Barn Owls sometimes had a second winter brood but I had assumed it was too rare to be true. Like a naive bird nerd, I sat outside the tree for over an hour, praying that a white face would poke out and greet me. Being one of the most timid birds in all of Britain, it was no wonder that nothing came out again. The one moment of seeing a wild owl in my garden and I missed it. Gutted.

'Hope springs eternal' as they say, and to my complete surprise, as the new year rolled around, that fleeting sighting became a regular occurrence. A naturally wary bird, sightings were very irregular but backed up by reports from neighbours. This became far from a one-off. Having alerted the Suffolk Wildlife Trust, who sent a team of Barn Owl experts to the tree, it transpired that there was a nest with chicks! To my dismay, the cavity was too deep for the ringers to reach, so I never actually saw a chick in the flesh.

Incredibly, the owls returned the next summer, but this was the year that it all changed. The days of fleeting glimpses were over and made way for some of the most bonkers encounters you could imagine.

Upon fledging, the chicks would line up along the fence right outside my window and happily play around. The local Sparrows must have been scared out of their lives. These owl chicks would also scratch at my window at 5am, not quite my most desired wake-up call. I'd poke my camera round the curtain and they would barely flinch. They would fly across the fields in the pouring rain, despite famously not having waterproof feathers. They would glide right above my head as I sat on the trampoline, I felt like a giant vole. The most elusive of all birds became as bold as brass. For at least another summer, my private owl show was popcorn worthy every night.

The following year was my last in the house so I never got to see if it was another bumper year for the barnies. The fact is, my particular story does not have a happy ending.

A year after moving away, I happened to go past the tree on the bus and despite motoring past, I knew in the pit of my stomach that the owls would not return. The side branches that the owls used to land on had been stripped bare, leaving a vast exposed trunk. I recently reacquainted myself with my neighbour who confirmed that they had not seen an owl visit the tree since I left.

Wildlife encounters scarcely come more in depth than this, and it has shaped my continued passion for conservation long into the future. This was just one tree in amongst thousands of now bustling Barn Owl nests. Their populations have survived a nationwide crash I hope that my little ash tree helped in some way. What a bizarre but brilliant Barn Owl nest.

Jack is an Environmental Studies graduate from the University of Kent, where he studied in the Durrell Institute of Conservation and Ecology. Creator of *Balcony Bird-Brain Blogs*, Jack is a UK wildlife lover with a particular fondness for birds. He resides in Essex, though originally hails from Norfolk. You can discover more of Jack's writing about his experiences with the natural world at: balconybirdbrain.blogspot.com

18

BACKYARD CONSERVATION

Steve Wood

Someone once said that they liked what I was doing with 'Backyard Conservation'. It took me by surprise, as I had never heard the term before.

I live in a beautiful, rural area, surrounded by mountains and forest. I am aware of how privileged I am to live in such a place. I also realise that many in the community do not share my privilege. I have acres of property, whereas many people have minimal or no green spaces, or may live in an unsafe area, where going outside is not an option. This may present a barrier to getting involved in an appreciation for nature – so how do we remedy that?

I have always believed that you can create future conservationists by helping people to appreciate the complexity of the world around them. It is important to take a look around outside, keep your eyes on the ground, observe the plants, or the sky, and see what's there.

My personal connection started with exploring the wildlife on my property; the diversity of life in my six acres is amazing. Over time, I've realised too that observing, cataloguing, and simply appreciating the life around me, can inspire others to get outside and look around too.

My focus has always been community education – to reach people who have a passing relationship with wildlife, or are curious about what lives around them. The term 'backyard conservation' has helped me to make sense of things. Those two words have helped me to reflect on what I'm doing, and how I could contribute to the bigger picture of environmentalism, conservation and wildlife protection.

It's a philosophy that has helped to inspire my online project, The Backyard Zoologist. Although there have been times where I have questioned the value of focusing solely on local wildlife, the principle of 'Backyard Conservation' has helped me to see the connection with the bigger picture of protecting our planet's wild spaces. I must continue to remind myself that there is a much bigger world out there, and what may be common to me, can be extraordinary and exotic to the global audiences that social media affords us.

'Backyard Conservation' may not seem as mighty, or impressive, or indeed daunting as actions like: 'environmentalism', 'climate change' or 'environmental justice', but these are all very big topics and they are not always easy for people to get involved with, or wrap their heads around.

What is easy to do for the planet, however, is to simply be good to the space you live in – whether it is tiny or giant. Let the species that reside there flourish. Keep it clean. Learn about what lives in your space, why it is there, and how it interconnects to the rest of the world.

The reality is, making the most simple connection with nature can inspire you. Any activity that fosters an appreciation for the natural world is a contribution to the bigger movements. That is Backyard Conservation, and you can do it!

My challenge is for all of you to encourage the people you know to get outside and enjoy the world, even if it is once a month or once a week. The more time you spend outdoors, the more time you take to appreciate what's out there, and the better off we all are. Get outside and check out a cool rock, a tree, budding spring flowers, birds, bugs, whatever it is that catches your eye. Simple observations foster a desire to know more – as proven time and time again through the work of science. Indeed, is it not the desire to enhance the community's knowledge that leads many to choose science as a career?

Backyard Conservation is also about passing your discoveries on. Start a social media account, talk about your experiences, write something – start somewhere. Share your observations, discoveries, and your wonder about the natural world. It is profound and it changes lives. Our knowledge, photographs, artwork and our passion can inspire people to join in, to venture outside, and to explore the world.

Backyard Conservation is also about becoming a caretaker for life. Every life is important. Wildlife is not here to serve some purpose for humans. It deserves protection, conservation, and most of all appreciation. Be a caretaker for your piece of the world. Every inch of green matters. Explore your local environment, no matter how big or small. I hope to do my bit to make this place that I occupy a cleaner, safer place for everyone and everything. Be kind to the Earth, and you will find that it rewards you with amazing things.

Steve Wood aka The Backyard Zoologist is a heavily tattooed, punk-rock-loving zoologist living on a rural mountain in Central New York State. Steve has been fascinated by wildlife (and dinosaurs!) since childhood. After working various careers, he went back to college in his 40s and earned a degree in Zoology, which brought him to various wildlife education jobs. See Backyard Conservation in action over at: instagram.com/thebackyardzoologist

19

BY THE SIDE
OF THE ROAD

Kayleigh Brookes

You may be surprised to hear that one sunny June day last year, I spent a wonderful couple of hours in a road verge!

When managed in a nature-friendly way, road verges can be absolutely amazing for wildlife. The flowers, insects and birds I encountered that day were fascinating, numerous and varied. This particular verge was wonderfully wide, and sloped up and away from the road. The top flattened out and most of it had, happily, been left unmown, leaving what was practically a small meadow! It was beautiful – a colourful carpet of life, painted with the yellows, whites and pinks of bird's-foot trefoil, oxeye daisies, red clover, and, my personal favourite, bee orchids.

It was mesmerising in there. So many insects were drawn to the flowers – butterflies, beetles, flies and bees all vying for nectar; the bees with pockets of pollen weighing down their hind legs. Various birds kept flitting out of the line of trees behind my mini-meadow, grabbing some insect or other and flashing back again, no doubt feeding their young.

I was lucky enough to witness a rather dramatic instance of this. As I watched an insect hovering above the herbage, trying to work out what it was – it had wings like a dragonfly but wasn't big enough to fit this ID – a magpie swooped in from stage left and snatched the unprepared insect from the sky, flying away with it, without so much as a pause or change of direction! I couldn't take a photo as it was so fast, but the memory will certainly remain with me!

Although the verge was beside a dual carriageway and a roundabout, I was able to tune out the drone of the traffic and focus on the abundance of nature all around me. Immersed in my newly beloved verge, I crawled around for a long time, becoming a part of the landscape and enjoying the profusion of life. Wildlife highlights included Red-Tailed Bumblebees, Hairy Shieldbugs, Seven-Spot Ladybirds, Marbled White Butterflies and Welsh Chafer Beetles.

These beetles were the funniest – they would climb to the top of a blade of grass, and when they got to the tip, their weight would cause the blade to bend over, leaving them hanging onto it upside down! Invariably this ended in the poor bug falling to the ground in a flurry of wings and wing cases. However, it didn't seem to deter them from scrambling back up to try again.

Quite by chance I managed to witness three different stages of a ladybird's life cycle. There were several adult Seven-Spot Ladybirds in the area, and I had also seen a couple of nymphs. The best bit was somehow spotting an adult on a blade of grass in front of a clutch of eggs she must have only just laid! This seemed to be an ideal spot for these striking red beetles.

I thoroughly enjoyed my time in the verge-meadow, enthralled by the wildlife around me. It was wonderful to be down on the ground, up close to so many incredible species, and it was a privilege to observe their lives. When managed with nature in mind, and only mown once a year – rather than incessantly – road verges are fantastic habitats for wildlife. They are also green corridors that enable species to move and migrate to other areas of suitable habitat.

You can show your support for wildlife-rich road verges by writing to your local council, or signing the petition by Plantlife calling for wildlife-friendly road verge management.

Kayleigh Brookes is a nature writer, conservationist and campaigner. She enjoys sharing her passion for wildlife and inspiring others with stories, information and poetry. Find out more at: kayleighannwriting.wordpress.com

20

PUBLIC RIGHTS OF WAY

Charlotte Ditchburn

Connecting with nature means accessing the great outdoors, we do this via public rights of way, open access land and nature reserves. We pass along riverbanks, over mountains, through woodlands and across the countryside and I have found my vocation in championing access to enable everyone to access nature through rights of way.

I have connected with nature since childhood. Having been brought up in the Lake District, I love the thrill of wild swimming and spending a night solo in my tent on the fells. I was a cub and a scout, which took me to many amazing places in nature, as well as completing my Bronze, Silver and Gold Duke of Edinburgh awards – which gave me a rooted love of the outdoors.

I found nature essential for my mental health later in life, when I found myself being diagnosed with post-traumatic stress disorder, anxiety and depression. My experiences in nature helped me to rebuild my confidence and psychological well-being, beginning with daily walks and slowly finding my feet for bigger adventures again. In a time when being around people felt extremely difficult and stressful, nature was there providing a reassuring safe space to let my emotions out and learn to heal myself. I was comforted by nature allowing me to process my feelings and problems in a space where the wildlife carried on, even when my own personal world felt like it was crumbling around me. Being immersed in nature enabled me to reduce the physical triggers of my mental health issues and it gave me a way of developing coping mechanisms for more stressful environments of everyday life.

Over time, I discovered group activities in nature, such as paddleboarding. Throughout the Covid-19 pandemic, when nature was more important than ever, it was vital to continue enjoying these kinds of activities outdoors, connecting with others when many of us faced loneliness.

There is now a body of scientific evidence showing just how essential nature is for our well-being. Green and blue spaces played a crucial role in our physical and mental well-being through the pandemic; it brought the issue of access to open space to the foreground of public consciousness. Some of us were confined to the four walls of our homes whilst the more privileged in society had access to nature and open air in their gardens.

I now work in the access sector to promote and secure the provision, protection, and preservation of rights of way and of access for ridden and driven horses over public roads, highways, footpaths, bridleways, carriageways, public paths, and other land. In England and Wales, we have access to roam freely around a mere 8% of the countryside and 3% of rivers.

With the 2026 deadline threatening over 49,000 miles of footpaths and many more miles of bridleways and byways, I am passionate about preserving these historic routes and making sure they are legally recorded before the cut-off date. I am a true cartophile and love studying historic and modern-day maps to find any discrepancies and find the routes that could be extinguished after 2026. These routes provide access for all users who will benefit greatly from accessing nature, they allow everyone, and not only those privileged enough to own outdoor spaces.

I hope that together, we can gain greater access rights to the land and waterways, and educate the public about the responsibilities we have to the countryside: its ecology, its communities, and its owners.

Charlotte Ditchburn works in the access sector, and blogs about Public Rights of Way and all things outdoors on her blog: *Public Rights of Way Explorer.* **She is an Ordnance Survey GetOutside Champion, an ambassador for the** *National Outdoor Expo* **and an ambassador for** *Active Suffolk*'**s 'This Girl Can' Suffolk campaign, inspiring and empowering women to get active. In the past she has worked as a Public Rights of Way Officer and is passionate about making the outdoors accessible for all. You'll normally find her outside walking, horse riding, paddleboarding, cycling or just taking in the views.**

21

MY JOURNEY
AS A NATURALIST

Harriet Day

The addiction to nature started young, when my dad would take me fishing at the weekends. I'll never forget the first time I saw a Kingfisher – the thrill of that electric-blue flash darting past has never left my mind. I was only young, but that exciting encounter awoke something within me. From that day onwards, I would beg my dad to always take me with him on his fishing trips.

Although the years have passed, my love for birds has remained – and developed into something even stronger. I have swapped fishing trips for the adventure of being a trainee bird ringer for the British Trust for Ornithology (BTO). Every weekend I join my trainer, Kevin, and the Sorby Breck Ringing Group, for a 4am gathering to safely catch birds.

Placing a small, lightweight metal ring gently on the bird's leg, there's something quite mesmerising about the mix of letters and numbers that will be used to relocate this individual when it migrates in the near future. Each ring has its own secret code that will teach us more about each fascinating species through the behaviour of each bird.

Last October I was fortunate enough to do a little bird ringing at Bempton Cliffs and Flamborough Head – two of East Yorkshire's most popular reserves, and well-known hotspots for migrating birds. I was in for a big surprise that morning at Flamborough, when I gently extracted a 5.6-gram Goldcrest from the mist net to find that it was already wearing a shiny new ring, inscribed with Norway!

To think that this tiny bird, which weighed about the same as a 20 pence coin, had taken flight across the North Sea just 48 hours earlier – managing to avoid predators, exhaustion and the risk of being lost – put things into perspective for me. So many challenges had been overcome in order to reach England, in the name of finding food and the optimum conditions for rearing offspring.

It is often said that way leads on to way, and just like my Kingfisher sighting had inspired my journey into bird ringing, my Goldcrest encounter inspired me begin making nest boxes. The nest boxes I have worked on are intended for Tawny Owls and Little Owls; two species whose population numbers are potentially on the decline.

Building nest boxes has seen me working with local farmers and landowners to gain access and permission to distribute the boxes across their land. This is my first year of working on this fulfilling project, so I would like to think that by next April we might have some owlets in the nest box, giving us the opportunity to weigh and measure them – and of course adorn them with their very own lightweight ring, with it special code to help monitor the population.

April is one of my favourite times of the year, the time when I head out and watch nature at its best; the trees are blooming, the frogs are spawning and the Chiffchaffs are singing. I get so excited to set my trail camera up in my local area to watch the hedgehogs awaken for food, as well as the squirrels digging up their winter snacks – or heading out with my bat detector in the late evenings, to try and make new records for my county. Not to mention that instant standstill you come to when seeing a beautiful splash of colour fluttering through the air... yes, you guessed it, the butterfly!

Well, this is me: a person that loves to be outdoors with my binoculars, exploring nature and capturing it through the lens, then writing about my incredible experiences. I will always explore, love, respect and protect nature, and I love sharing that experience with other people too. I hope that I can help to encourage the next generation to embrace nature; for it to bring them the fulfilment and happiness that it constantly gives for me. Nature is the gift that keeps on giving.

Harriet Day is a naturalist and environmentalist with a lust for experiencing the wonder of wildlife. She never turns down the opportunity to go out bird ringing, or exploring with her camera and binoculars. After finding a love for nature writing, blogging, and podcasting, she has had some of her work published in *Birdwatching Magazine*, has created a podcast for the *River Trust* and written on the *BTO Blog*, raising awareness for mental health issues. In her spare time, she makes nest boxes and feeders for birds and tries to work with schools to help educate the younger generation on where to find wildlife.

22

THE MOORLAND FAIRGROUND

Alicia Hayden

When the wind calls you to the moors, you can't resist, can't say no – not for a moment.

Her hair whips around her as she runs, weaving through the heather which pricks at her legs – tripping on the burnt stumps and roots. She had heard the rumours, the whispers about the wind calling you. Some said it called for you when it was lonely, others said it called when it had something to show.

Shoes thudding into the peatbog, mud splashing up to her calves – she's never really been one for rural legends, but the moorland wind – that is something worth believing in. The wind ruffles her hair like an old friend as she gasps for breath, at peace on the moor at last. She sinks onto a tuffet behind her, ready to be shown why she's here.

The booming, bubbling, shrieking, wailing calls of a dozen moorland birds commences, whirling into an orchestra which swells with the wind's whistling – an intricate, eerie melody which fills the air in the same way a warm stew bubbles up in a casserole dish. It is comfortable, and it feels like coming home. Snipe burbling up and down like tuneful yo-yos, and Lapwings swinging around each other like ice dancers in the sky – the moorland has become a playground for wildlife and wilderness. A fairground for water and wind, feathers and fur, heather and gorse.

The tuffets and heather around her twitch as a hare peeks its nose tentatively out, and slowly the rest of its golden fur follows, until it is peacefully munching through stems, long ears pricking at the slightest foreign rustle on the breeze. Further along mice and voles scamper like jet-propelled toffees through wavering grass, and a family of Short-Eared Owls test out their wings and hunting skills by following the weaving trails.

She watches, her eyes growing wider with every rustle, every song, every new creature joining the fairground. She is holding her breath with anticipation: what will come next?

The Curlew's cry lights up the sky, splitting the calm lull like a lightning bolt. Tawny-speckled wings sailing through the morning sunlight – it can go anywhere it desires, yet it chooses to drift in front of her, as if asking her, "Will you join us?"

Her feet are moving before she realises what's happening, and she's running along the old moor paths, setting up clouds of dozing moths and spiders scuttling into their burrows. Soft purples, twinkling yellows, gentle greens splash through her vision like paint, and the song of wildlife rises around her like multicoloured wings. She is so happy, she feels she could fly, and join the Curlew on its journey through the morning.

When she returns home, the evening moon is peeping over the horizon, bathing the woods and the outskirts of the moor in a creamy light. She hesitates before going in, aware that the wind may not call her to the moor again – this may have been her one chance to see the fairground, to hear the orchestra.

The stars twinkle down at her in their all-knowing way, and she suddenly realises why the wind only ever calls you once to the moor. Because it only needs to show you once.

Alicia Hayden is an award-winning wildlife photographer, artist, writer, and film-maker from North Yorkshire, currently studying Biological Sciences at Oxford University. Her debut illustrated wildlife poetry book *Rain before Rainbows* is out now. 50% of profits from the sale of her poetry collection go to the wildlife hospital Tiggywinkles. Find out more at: aliciahaydenwildlifephotography. zenfolio.com

23

FOREST SONG

Nick Stephenson

Walking to your heaven,
stairway to the moon.
Night captures a strange rapture,
forest fires in June.

Light trickles out the windows
before the hour is late.
Fireflies dim and flicker
and light up every movement on your face.

Head buzzing like a garden,
pools of dreams and signs.
Soft lilting syrup evening,
a trip that sails so high.

Snow walker, winter cover,
I know you understand.
Hiding out, there's no doubt,
the gentle trees will part like desert sand.

Part like desert sand.

'Forest Song' is the lyrics to a song of the same name, by Nick Stephenson.

Nick Stephenson's wildlife storytelling takes the form of music; he is a singer-songwriter with a passion for nature and wildlife. His playlist 'Songs of Nature' is available to listen to on Soundcloud.

He released a fundraising single 'Poor Little Boy' in 2019 for One Man's Rescue campaign, which provides senior dogs in rescue centres with fun days out. Find out more at: nickfstephenson.com

24

ALL WALKS OF WILDLIFE

Rhiannon Irving

It was as I walked alongside my father down a muddied path studded with early bluebells and gauzy cow parsley that I realised my connection with nature is embedded deeply in my relationship with family.

That my ability to recognise the Reed Bunting in front of me with its black cap, bib and notched tail, from the House Sparrow with its grey crown and white cheeks, was a skill afforded to me by my parents, a consequence of the omnipresent bird prints lining the walls of our home, the wildlife guides shelved close by. That the happiness and peace nature brings me as an adult is a result of the kindred spirits I find in them, of my young mind overwhelmed with a passion and wonder for nature, of a childhood crowded with wildlife.

Images linger in my distant memory, of sheep grazing in the late twilight sun at the fringe of New Forest moorland, the ground carpeted in swathes of purple heather, spiny gorse and flames of bird's-foot trefoil. Sitting with my father in the dusky evening light in the garden of our childhood home, watching the zip and dive of bats catching insects on the wing, sat in silence absorbing the hush, yet feeling the shared awe flowing between us; the tendrils of buzzy excitement as each bat flits overhead. Watching fox cubs play on the nearby field, the sky darkening from the golden vibes of sunset to inky blackness without us realising, our vision adjusting to absorb the scene for as long as possible.

Away from the familiar English countryside and a frisson of expectation whilst horse riding through the pine-needle-padded ground of Yellowstone National Park with my mother, seeing the conifers scored by black bears, the tense knowledge of a world of wildlife hidden just out of view. Watching bison crop the vast grassland landscape, prairie dogs standing to attention amongst their volcano-like burrow entrances; all pitched beneath the shadow of Devils Tower, with the stacked, amber-coloured cliffs towering like a border to the horizon.

Lying alongside her on the deck of a boat as dolphins surge and pitch across the Tenerife water, whipping up white sea foam underneath a scorching sun.

My first nature connections made without my family are in Ecuador and the Galápagos Islands, the buzz of hummingbirds in the dense, hazy cloud forest and the courtship choreography of the Blue-Footed Boobys accompanied by the repetitive snap of my camera. A camera lent to me by my father, a symbolic echo of how I came to be here, that this experience is shared despite the physical distance.

Older yet, my parents by my side as I graduate with a Zoology degree, the implicit knowledge that I am this inspired, energised, motivated by the natural world because of them, that my life has taken this path because they gave me a childhood surrounded by nature; that I am grateful and incredibly lucky they nurtured me this way and that I had these opportunities.

As nature continues its circle of life, so do I, moving away from home yet sending messages and photos whenever I see something that excites me. An unexpected Hen Harrier buffeted by the breeze and its blur of a skydance means a phone call to my father, images sent to him from nature reserves that we will soon visit together, grainy photographs I've snapped that require his identification expertise, every nature experience I have is a connection to my family regardless of being apart. And when we do see each other again, we are the mirror image of each other holding our cameras steady on a post to photograph a handsome Heron or regal Red Deer, watching nature unfurl around us as if we were never apart.

My daughter arrives and the world is truly unlocked to me, the opportunity to share this family passion for nature as if it is an heirloom I can pass to her. Her face glows with the colours of the ochre autumn leaves, calling out to the birds that flutter above our heads on our walks, each moment she has in nature only a fragment of what she has yet to experience.

Held in her grandad's arms and wide-eyed at the ducks swimming idly across the lake, my heart overwhelmed with the love I feel for my family and the intertwined connection I have for nature, accrued in a series of seemingly inconsequential moments.

A love and connection I can continue to infuse into every moment we spend together. Pure reverence for nature and boundless curiosity flowing through me from them, and now from me to my daughter, from a family connection to my connection to nature.

Rhiannon Irving has had a passion for wildlife since she was small, and has worked towards a wildlife-based career her entire life. She recently graduated with an MSc in Zoo Conservation Biology and started blogging to record her own experiences with wildlife and conservation, particularly her adventures with her baby daughter, as she introduces her to nature and the world around her. Read more at: allwalksofwildlife.com

25

THE BRITISH RIVER

Nick Wilson-Smith

The spring of 2020 marked a rather special occasion for me, surveying for the somewhat elusive Eurasian Otter. I had only ever spotted this majestic mammal once before, on the Scottish Isle of Colonsay. It was without a doubt one of those life-altering experiences, which will be forever etched in my memory. For some time, I was able to sit nearby, with my binoculars fixed on a mother and cub diving for salmon on the shores of Balnahard Beach. Truly one of those unforgettable wildlife encounters.

Despite such an incredible encounter, it had still bothered me that I was yet to see an inland otter, coursing through our rivers and – for someone who generally spends a lot of time on riverbanks exploring their sights and sounds – this was now becoming be a real bugbear of mine. I have always been drawn to riparian habitats for the tranquility and green vibrancy that they bring, and hoped one day to couple it with an otter sighting. The perfect pairing of landscape and beast.

Rising at the crack of dawn, I ventured down to my local river, the Ouseburn, in anticipation of a rare sighting. I mapped out the survey sites, took photos, checked everywhere for signs of the fabled jasmine-scented spraint, tracks, feeding remains and, yes, anal jelly. Nothing. Not a jot. Even though for me, the area looked perfect condition-wise, with good water quality and surrounding habitat.

They are seen fairly regularly along this stretch, by otter standards at least. Alas, it just wasn't meant to be. So, I left that Sunday morning feeling disappointed, but in all honesty not surprised. I recorded my negative presence data and that was that. Or at least, so I thought.

That afternoon, I decided to go for a walk at work. The site was closed due to lockdown, so I was quite literally a lone ranger. As always, I subconsciously directed myself to the riverside walk. Thinking nothing of it, I took my usual route hoping to see some of its regular inhabitants: Dippers, Kingfishers, Grey Herons, and with a bit of luck the occasional Mandarin Duck.

Out of nowhere, I heard a huge splash in the nearside margin and half expected it would be a noisy Mallard, or perhaps even the much-maligned American Mink. Not this time.

As I rushed over, an otter briefly resurfaced, before rapidly submerging and corkscrewing right past me, just under the water's surface. I managed to get a clear glimpse of its webbed paws, but that was about it. Nothing could be more typical of this aloof animal, than to carry out hours of survey work the whole weekend long, capturing nothing, then go on a spontaneous jaunt and see one immediately without even trying. It made my day, and I couldn't help but laugh at the good fortune. A reward for my efforts perhaps? Maybe, but I still left feeling slightly frustrated that the opportunity to sit and watch otters on a river at my own pace hadn't yet presented itself. I craved more.

Keep the faith, I reminded myself. Nature never disappoints, and perseverance always prevails.

Now well into May, it was a scorching day at work and I was carrying out my regular site patrol loop. I parked up on the woodland edge and started meandering down to the river, past my favourite alder, which was now surrounded by stitchwort, red campion, wood cranesbill and butterbur.

Thankfully, on this occasion I had a camera around my neck, or I'm not entirely convinced that my colleagues would have believed what I witnessed next. There it was, right in front of me, not three metres away! Bold as brass, a sow otter and cub swimming in tandem.

Forgetting about my camera all together at this point, I was overcome by a combination of sheer disbelief and utter joy. The mother led the cub back to the tree base holt quickly, before re-entering the water to put on a real show. I watched her for an hour, as she swam back and forth catching Brown Trout and Grayling. She was fully aware of my presence, as I crouched down on the bank, but didn't seem interested or remotely intimidated. Adding to my amazement, this was two o'clock in the afternoon.

I couldn't get enough of this display of supreme confidence, from such a flawlessly skilled predator. This was the epitome of wildlife watching. Eventually, I decided to leave her be and drag myself away from the moment, respecting the spectacle that she had duly delivered. I had finally clapped eyes on the holy grail of the quintessential British river. After being within almost touching distance of, until this day, the rather evasive *Lutra lutra*, I will forever be in her debt.

Nick Wilson-Smith works and studies as a budding ranger in North East England, for a large conservation charity. He created his blogging website as a celebration of nature, magical wildlife encounters and a place to express a love of mother nature through his own snaps and scribblings. Visit: naturalistnick.co.uk

26

ENCOUNTERING THE QUEEN OF THE SOUTH AFRICAN COAST

Hannah Rudd

Few past experiences could have prepared me for what I was on the verge of facing. Looking out across the calm harbour, with the gentle white horses hugging the rocky Gansbaai shoreline, I could observe ocean for as far as my eyes could see. The auburn sun was gradually rising across the horizon and the sky was soon filled with a mesmerising array of autumnal tones. All around me people were hectically running around, preparing both the cage-diving boats and the tourists for the trip ahead, yet an overwhelming feeling of tranquility consumed me.

Breathing in the crisp ocean air in the early hours of a chilly Wednesday morning, I couldn't wait to get out there and be surrounded by endless blue. As I climbed the stairs to board the banana-yellow hull of the 'Shark Team' I felt the blood coursing through my veins with anticipation more quickly than ever before. Excited chatter engulfed the air as animated visitors discussed their expectations and their journey to this very moment. For many, our voyage had been a dream since being a young child and felt like a pilgrimage of sorts. As an aspiring marine scientist, I was on the brink of undoubtedly making one of the most momentous first encounters of my career.

Travelling across Van Dyks Bay towards Dyer Island, we charged through the building swell, which became more powerful the further we ventured away from the shoreline. There is something so exhilarating about being on the ocean and all around me were people with childlike grins emblazoned across their mottled cheeks. Despite the bone-chillingly cold conditions, and the odd bout of seasickness, there was an overwhelming sense of fulfilment in the air.

When we finally moored a few hundred metres offshore, at a site known as Jouberts Dam to the locals, there was a flurry of anticipation as the crew worked tirelessly to get the large metallic cage suspended in the water and fixed to the starboard side of the boat.

Whilst expending substantial energy myself in a bid to frantically hoist my wetsuit on, I couldn't help but notice how close we were to the shoreline. Pearly Beach was right there in front of us. A beautiful expanse of glorious white sands, a renowned local swimmers' beach, and undoubtedly a popular tourist destination during the summer months. But there was no time for wonderment, it was the moment I had been waiting for since late childhood.

Enthusiastically, I threw my legs over the side of the hull, slipping down into the metal cage and the ice-cold waters that were there to greet me. Grasping the frozen bars above me, I clenched my fists to secure myself in place.

Frantically taking one large breath and thrusting my body deep down into the waters, I mustered every bit of strength I had to battle the strong current. Once consumed by the bitterly cold sea, I began desperately searching to catch a glimpse of the ginormous fish I had travelled all this way to see. After a few moments, there she was. A majestic, four-metre long female emerged from the murky abyss and inquisitively looked us all in the eye, one by one.

Clampy, named so because of the hole in her dorsal fin from a previous satellite tracking tag, effortlessly glided past us all. She was not aggressive. She was not fear-inducing. Instead, she was the exact opposite of many preconceptions the average person you may meet on the street would have about sharks. Calm, inquisitive and ever so slightly shy.

There is something so magical about meeting *Carcharodon carcharias*, colloquially known as the Great White Shark, for the first time. Whether it was the icy cold waters of Van Dyks Bay or the sheer majesty you gain from looking one of the ocean's most magnificent animals right in the eyes, I had never felt more wonderment in my whole life. If seeing an African lion roam the savannah is the pinnacle of terrestrial wildlife watching, then witnessing a Great White Shark glide across the pelagic was the marine equivalent.

Thinking about it, both Clampy and I were both gazing directly at one of the most formidable predators on Earth. In that moment that I locked eyes with Clampy, I didn't feel a sense of panic or endangerment, simply an appreciation of the sheer grandeur with which this animal graces our oceans and the integral role it plays in marine ecosystem health. In that same moment, my heart was heavy at the thought of my children not being able to bear witness to the ruler of the high seas.

Hannah Rudd is a marine biologist, science communicator and photographer. She is a member of the *Youth For Our Planet* group and a *WWF Changemaker*, and launched *Leading Women in Marine Science* to explore the representation of women in the science. Hannah's passion for sharks has taken her across the world from researching Whale Sharks in the Maldives to studying Great White

Sharks in South Africa. Combining this with her love of writing, in 2022 her first book will be published with Bloomsbury Publishing on UK seas and how we can all do our bit to save them. Find out more at: hannahrudd.com

27

I SHOULD BE SCARED OF YOU

Claire Edwards

I should be scared of you,
Your sheer, unmatched power and gigantic size.
My heart should be pounding,
But all I do is fall deeper into your amber eyes.
Like a visual magnet I can't break away.

In the wind your wiry auburn hairs stray
And your pink tongue above a whiskered white chin wet
From dribble laps at your mottled nose in a longing way.
Your round stare penetrates deep into my soul, and yet
At the same time, I couldn't guess what you'd like to say
If your voice was free to human words.

Fixed by your presence, you choose to humour me.
Relaxed back on your ochre, muscular legs undisturbed
You play with my goosebumped attention;
Not once revealing any intention,
Nor displaying the true predator you could be.

We both know you're beyond my apprehension
And you don't have to stay.
But you do.
And changed my life in every way.
The moment that connected me and you;
When I locked eyes with a lion king.

Claire Edwards has always adored animals, but it was only when she turned 30 and took part in a big cat close encounter that she realised her true calling was actually in this sector. She is a proud volunteer for The Big Cat Sanctuary in Kent and will soon begin a Masters degree in Animal Welfare Science, Ethics and Law.

28

LIVING 'THE DREAM'

Beth Jennings

Under the heat of the African sun I prepared for a hard day of work – bottle feeding, cuddling, bathing and playing with lion cubs. I thought I was living the dream, but this was only the beginning of my worst nightmare. I knew not to swim with dolphins, not to ride an elephant and not to visit a tiger sanctuary in Thailand, but I was never warned about another industry, currently booming, and fuelled by lies.

In South Africa, thousands of volunteers and tourists like myself are sold the same experience under the guise of conservation; the chance to help hand-rear orphaned lion cubs in preparation for release into the wild. I volunteered in 2015 and within days I realised that the trip had been mis-sold and I had been lied to by the travel agency and the park itself.

There are an estimated 297 lion breeding parks in South Africa, around a third of which offer cub interactions to the public. The number of lions in captivity is thought to be between 6,000 and 8,000 although estimations also reach as high as 10,000. In comparison there are only 20,000 wild lions left in the world, a huge drop from 200,000 in the 1940s. So where are the captive bred lions really going?

Within South Africa, canned hunting is entirely legal and somewhat encouraged. A canned hunt is a trophy hunt within a fenced enclosure, ensuring success for the hunter. As well as physical constraints, the lions are often hand-reared and habituated to humans, therefore see no reason to flee.

Regular trophy hunts can take up to 21 days with no guaranteed kill, whereas with a canned hunt, you can choose a lion from a menu and be in and out in the same day. An act so deplorable, even trophy hunters are speaking out against it.

Another industry currently booming within South Africa is the trade in lion bone. The South African government has issued an annual quota of 1,500 lion skeletons to be legally exported to Asia, for use in traditional medicines. The government claim that in doing so, they are protecting wild populations, however, they are yet to provide any scientific evidence to prove this.

It is also impossible to tell a captive-bred lion skeleton apart from a wild, poached one, so there is no way to guarantee which bones are being exported. Across Asia, the bones are being made into wine or "cakes" that supposedly have healing properties and are sometimes sold to consumers as tiger bone.

The reality of handling lion cubs or walking with lions in South Africa is that they will never be released into glorious, wild reserves. They will be hunted – their heads hung as a trophy and their bones crushed into cake.

All too often I receive messages from volunteers assuring me that the park they visited has "no involvement" with hunting. However, this is false. There is absolutely no benefit to hand-rearing lion cubs and volunteers should not be paying thousands to do so. Absolutely no park that offers hands-on interactions is ethical – no exceptions.

Once I discovered that the cubs I had bonded with would meet such a dreadful fate I launched a blog, *Claws Out*, to share my experience and educate potential volunteers about the "con" within these conservation parks. As a volunteer with first-hand experience of the lies and deceit, my story was picked up by other NGOs (non-governmental organisations) and politicians resulting in articles, interviews and even a speech in European Parliament alongside MEPs.

My story began with my passion for big cats which led me to book what I believed would be the trip of a lifetime – but returning to the UK, I was committed to raising awareness through my experience. Through my blog I was invited to feature in magazines and newspapers across the world and I now devote my time and passion to making a difference within lion welfare.

Beth Jennings is the founder of *Claws Out*, and a staunch campaigner for lion welfare. In 2018 she partnered with Born Free Foundation and Olsen Animal Trust to produce a short film based on her experience called *Claws Out: The Truth About Cub Petting*. Find out more at: claws-out.com

29

JUNGLE SCHOOL

Kate Williams

In 2019, I travelled to Borneo to visit the Borneo Orangutan Survival Foundation and spend time shadowing their vets.

It was made clear to me from the beginning that no contact with the orangutans was allowed unless in a veterinary capacity or if they initiated it themselves.

Rather than any sense of disappointment, this was a relief to me, as it proved that the organisation had the orangutans' best interests at heart. This no-contact rule is to give them the best chance of being reintroduced back into the wild and also protects them from contracting anthropozoonotic (diseases transmissible from a human to an animal) as much as possible.

The tale of how these orphans came to be at the centre is an extremely sad one. All of them orphans, all had lost their mothers through either hunting, human–animal conflict or confiscation from the illegal pet trade. The sheer volume of baby orangutans came as a shock to me, and proved just how much the orangutan as a species needs our help.

The normal routine for the orangutan orphans was to go to Jungle School in the daytime, where they were separated into classes based on their age and ability. Here, they learned all the things that their mother would have taught them in the first six or seven years of their lives. This included how to climb trees, what fruits to eat and what predators to avoid.

After school everyday, around 4pm, the orangutans came lolloping out of the jungle and back to the centre, where they played in the playground for around half an hour before being put to bed in their enclosures.

One particular afternoon when they were busy playing after school, an enormous thunderstorm started to rumble and the heavens opened. The rain pounded down and the orangutans were visibly anxious by the hostile turn in the weather. The minders tried to shepherd the orangutans to their enclosures a little earlier than anticipated to find shelter.

I was leaning on the veterinary building watching the commotion from a distance when little Winnie started coming over to me. She stopped at my feet and hugged my legs, looking up at me with those big, soulful eyes. Then after a moment, she climbed up my body wanting to be carried back to bed. Her head on my shoulder and her arms wrapped around me, just as a child would.

I suddenly realised this was a motherless animal, just wanting comfort in a moment of fear. It was one of the most amazing experiences of my life and something I'll never, ever forget.

Nonetheless, it was heartbreakingly sad that her mother was not there to do the job that I was doing. We must acknowledge why these orphans are here and take a long look at ourselves and ask what can be done to help our most precious of cousins.

Kate Williams is a wildlife vet. Her blog, *Vet Tales*, is about veterinary, wildlife and travel focused on the adventures she has had while gaining experience with wildlife. Kate shares some of the key conservation issues she has encountered along the way over at: vet-tales.com

30

THE DOMINANT MALE

Bella Lack

We stood in the warm twilight of Borneo, in the Sepilok Orangutan Rehabilitation Centre in Sabah. The orangutans had made their nests for the night and the piercing wails of the cicadas that started at sunset were slowly abating into a background throb of noise.

We were in a small group with one guide. We sat outside the orphan nursery on a damp slope, binoculars being passed round, pressed tightly to eyes and then passed on again. We were watching as the flying squirrels made their 'leap of faith'. They would come out from their nests and scurry up the tree until, with a sudden thrust, they would launch into the night, their large bodies silhouetted against the darkening sky.

This was when our group would let out a collective sigh of wonderment as we watched these cat-sized creatures elegantly soaring through the tangled canopy. It was then that we first heard it. The sound is unlike any other I had ever heard.

Dr Brigitte Spillmann has described it as 'a series of long booming pulses and grumbles, which can be heard through more than 1 km of dense jungle.' However, nothing can compare with the feeling of hearing this call. It reverberates through your body.

Upon hearing this, the guide whispered frantically into his walkie-talkie. Within moments, swarms of excitable guides were materialising, weaving their way through the trees with the nimbleness and grace that only experienced forest dwellers possess. We knew this was special. In the excitement, we soon interpreted that that the male had never been seen before. He was wild.

It is not unusual for a dominant male to leave his nest if he has been disturbed. Regretfully, he must have obviously felt unsettled by the throng of binocular-wielding apes that stood searching for flying squirrels and so he abandoned his nest and began to 'long call' in an attempt to dissuade us. If he had stayed quietly in his throne of leaves, we would have been unaware of the regal presence mere metres above us.

He soon came down, his eyes ablaze with the anger that any human will know if they have been disturbed from deep sleep. His flanges protruded from his cheeks. His body was massive, drenched in thick orange hair. His hands were easily larger than my head and we watched in admiration as this king of the jungle attempted to proceed towards us.

Fortunately, the shoots that he used to try and swing towards us were much too delicate for this mighty king. When his anger had heightened into a boiling rage, we were ushered away.

Yet, to this day, I can still see this indomitable being glaring at us through the foliage. It was an experience I could never forget.

Bella Lack is a young conservationist and wildlife campaigner. She has a strong social media presence, which she uses to educate and inspire others concerning global wildlife issues. She uses her Twitter account to help educate others on critical problems and encourage them to take action. She is an ambassador for Born Free Foundation and Jane Goodall's Roots and Shoots.

31

PROTECT WHAT
YOU LOVE

Rachael Barber

A chance encounter with a dolphin and I was hooked. My connection with wildlife started there and then, and my 6-year-old self wanted to 'work' with whales and dolphins. Fast-forward 31 years (yikes!) and here I am: a Marine Mammal Consultant with over 15 years of working in the marine mammal world.

I have worked as a guide on whale-watching boats, a surveyor onboard small yachts, giant ferries and classy cruise ships. Now, while desk-based, I provide advice to offshore industries on mitigating the impacts of noise on marine mammals.

Every opportunity I have, I try and get my 'blubber fix' whether that is in the UK or further afield.

I live in the middle of East Anglia and yet I have seen a Humpback Whale from the Norfolk coast, not to mention catching up with my Patronus (for all you Potter fans), the Harbour Porpoise, on numerous occasions from these eastern shores. I've seen British Orca, breaching Sperm Whales, stampeding Fraser's Dolphin and the rare and elusive Longman's Beaked Whale. I have smelled the breath of a Minke Whale and witnessed the majesty of the Blue Whale, to name but a few of the amazing encounters I have had. I feel my connection with whales and dolphins today is as strong as that first encounter all those years ago.

When I met my now husband, my connection to the natural world widened. Until then I was very focused, tunnel vision, on whales and dolphins. He opened my eyes to the world of birds. I learned to identify them, by sight and sound (still learning!) and I became a trained bird ringer contributing to the conservation of our birds.

In 2012, I began sharing my stories of wildlife with my family, and the Wild Barley blog was born. Through this, I told stories of adventures with birdwatching and ringing, and whale and dolphin watching of course. But there are also tales of fungi, fossils, amphibians, snakes, jungle exploits and African odysseys, travels near and far.

In 2015, I became a mummy. So many of my colleagues and friends seemed to give up, especially with bird ringing. But I was determined. I wanted to share my love and connection with wildlife with my daughter. And so, I took her along with me. From 3 weeks old I have taken my daughter to bird ringing sessions, out birdwatching, and even dolphin and whale watching. Don't get me wrong, it's hard, and I am more limited in what I can do – especially since becoming a mum for the second time in 2020 – but I am determined.

Sometimes I sit with a grumbly child and a crying baby, and wonder what on Earth I am doing; why am I putting us through this. But when I see their excitement and wonder I know I am giving them something priceless: a connection, respect and love for nature.

I love seeing my little girl's delight at holding a bird, and her knowledge of wildlife at such a young age astounds me. I cannot help but smile when I hear her squeals of delight as she pond dips, or goes rock pooling, filling the air with her million questions of 'what is it' and 'why'. I love how she plays 'nests and swans' or how she tells me the details of how she made a 'home' for a ladybird at school.

I love how she yells 'look Mummy, your favourite animal' when she sees an orca, how she helps Daddy identify the local swans and how she is delighted at feeding the ducks – she especially loves baby ducks, because they 'are soooo cute!'

Then there is my little boy, only just beginning on his wildlife adventures. Still, his little face creases up into a huge smile whenever he sees a bird, he points at them saying 'da da' and for a moment I thought his first word would be 'duck' until he did it to a car, the sky, a light, the dog, a toy, and then me!

Whatever my little ones grow up to be, whether it is a 'child bird ringer' or 'horse rider' (her words), or something completely different to nature, I just hope they keep that connection and respect for our natural world. After all, you protect what you love.

Rachael Barber is passionate about all wildlife, but whales and dolphins in particular. She completed a BSc in Zoology and an MSc in Applied Ecology and Conservation, and has worked for a few seasons as a guide on a whale-watch boat in Scotland, as well as on the ferry crossing the Bay of Biscay. In 2011, she became involved with Marine Mammal Observations and mitigation for offshore industries, and is now a Marine Mammal Consultant (as well as a mummy to two little people).

Rachael is also a trained bird ringer, catching and monitoring birds for the British Trust for Ornithology. She has been writing about her wildlife adventures on Wild Barley (named after her pup) for nearly 10 years. Read more at: wildbarley.co.uk

PART THREE
LIFELONG
CONNECTIONS

32
NATURE SPOTTING

Berenice Tregenna

I notice nature and feel connected to it wherever I am. I often find it in unlikely places – and that is because I am a nature spotter!

"Some see weeds; I see insect café"; I thought of this quote when I saw a line of dandelions at the end of my drive. There are so many plants that are seen as weeds which are vital to insects. The need to speak up for common plants and insects prompted me to start my blog called 'Berie Tree'.

Pavement plants growing up through the concrete are known to be a favourite of mine. I crouch down in the street with a camera to take photos of them. I even smile when I see moss highlighting the concrete like natural graffiti. There is also a very tall birch tree in my road that I have photographed at different angles. I see it as beautiful as I watch it changing through the seasons. Others just pass on by and never look up. The tree is invisible to them as they get on with their day.

I have been known to hover by a buddleia bush at the end of someone's garden, staring at the Painted Lady Butterflies. The people living there must have wondered why I was dawdling on the pavement outside their house. My 'butterfly loitering' seems to extend to car parks and other spaces. I have been known to watch and photograph a Red Admiral on an ivy bush outside a restaurant – more interested in watching this butterfly feeding than actually going indoors to feed myself!

You can imagine how slow I am at walking because I stop every few minutes to take a photo. My husband is often up ahead, patiently waiting for me to catch up. I always say, "I won't be long", but I do get carried away sometimes.

My grandad once told me that he sat down on a bench in the middle of a bustling town centre and all of a sudden looked up to see a group of birds overhead. He thought that he was the only person noticing the birds as everyone else was probably too busy to even look!

Perhaps it's his influence that means I look for wildlife wherever I am.

I like to look out of the window at birds as if my house is a giant hide. I have watched Blackbirds flitting in and out of their nest in my ivy, for example. I have seen Wood Pigeons coupled up on our fence. Spotting squirrels scurrying in the garden, too. In a previous job, I enjoyed watching a seagull nest with its little chicks right outside our office window which overlooked a rooftop.

I am an anxious person, who also has a chronic pain condition called fibromyalgia and I can honestly say that nature is my best medicine. It has a calming effect on me like nothing else. Just watching bees buzzing around my nettles can lift my mood and reduce my pain.

I want to inspire people to find time to look for nature and feel a connection with it. It's important not to just walk on by through life. There is so much out there that is overlooked and I like to bring it to everyone's attention.

The next time you go for a walk in the streets where you live, look out for the birds flitting about, the flowers in the pavement cracks and the trees waving in the wind. You might be surprised about how happy this natural connection makes you feel…

Berenice Tregenna runs the *Berie Tree* nature blog, which holds a magnifying glass up to common insects and plants. Her aim is to spread nature awareness and appreciation, encouraging people to do more to help the environment. Each post focuses on a certain insect or plant with a mixture of poems, photos, her own drawings and factual information. Berenice believes that both art and science can be blended together to engage others with their natural surroundings – this is the ethos of her blog, which can be found at: berrietree.wordpress.com

33

WILDLIFE WRITER

Chloe Petrylak

Ever since I can remember, I have been obsessed with wildlife. I was one of those kids who spent most of their time asking (what I'm sure my parents would have said were) the most impossible questions about our natural world.

From a very early age, I knew I wanted to spend my life doing something related to animals and the environment in some way, shape, or form. Having always loved the ocean, and after swimming with dolphins in Florida's Discovery Cove at the age of 10 (back when I didn't fully understand conservation and the differences between wild and captive animals), I desperately wanted to become a dolphin trainer. Witnessing the way in which they were able to glide through the water with ease, show a variety of emotions, and use their inquisitive minds to explore the world around them absolutely fascinated me. And that's where my passion for animals and our planet really took off.

Fast-forward 12 years or so, and here I was at the start of a wonderful, decade-long career as a wildlife writer and content creator, passionate about raising awareness and encouraging change. From working for *National Geographic Kids* magazine and *BBC Wildlife*, to writing my very own animal book; during this time I also had the pleasure of meeting Dr. Jane Goodall at various Roots & Shoots events, travelling to numerous countries to discover the wildlife that can be found there, and writing thousands of articles on everything from endangered species and newly discovered creatures, to climate change and coral bleaching.

Just before the pandemic began in 2020, my family moved into a new house. A few months into lockdown, similarly to many other people around the UK, we decided to start feeding the birds that visited our garden. We invested in a beautiful bird table and hanging bird-ball cage and, before we knew it, we were welcoming flocks of birds every single day. From various seeds and oats to crushed peanuts and dried mealworms, we researched and bought it all, ready for our new feathered friends to devour within seconds of me putting it all out.

From the comfort of our kitchen with my RSPB book and a pair of binoculars to hand, I have loved watching the birds swoop down. After a while, I noticed that they were starting to feel comfortable enough to continue feeding whilst I was sitting out in the garden. To be able to watch species such as Robins, Sparrows, Collared Doves and Starlings so closely is absolutely incredible and can really put you at peace.

As a result of these life experiences, my connection to wildlife has grown ever stronger, even if it hasn't quite turned out the way 10-year-old, dolphin-watching me had initially imagined. I know that I have been very fortunate in the opportunities I have been given and I'm extremely grateful to continue doing what I love.

Chloe Petrylak is a freelance writer, editor, and proofreader specialising in wildlife and the environment. She has worked for *National Geographic Kids UK*, *BBC Wildlife*, and *PetsRadar*, and is currently the social media manager for *Eco Kids Planet* magazine. You can find her work over at: chloemaywrites.com

34

AN ELEPHANT CHILD NO MORE

Will Travers

She had been caught as a child, an elephant child, dearly beloved. At the age of two (or maybe three) her family was gone and a new human 'family' formed around her.

The wild lands were replaced by a small, cosy, patch of Earth, surrounded by a wall, edged on one side by a road and on the other by a well-kept lawn leading to houses and the lodge.

And that was where she stayed – for 20 years. Her friends were few but constant. The monkey in the nearby cage, the man who came and called her name and fed her sugar cane and other treats.

If was a life, of sorts.

* * * *

The huge green truck was surrounded by strange people. It parked right up alongside the wall, and unloaded a huge, elephant-size box in front of the gate. The man came, and called and cooed, and tried to tempt her into the box that had been so carefully placed, chains a-jangling, but she refused. It didn't seem right.

So now she ended up in the box she never knew. But there it was. She looked out through the iron-girded roof as she swayed and clanged and bumped… and then, more gently, rocked from side to side as the scudding clouds overhead gave way to darkness. And she was still in the box.

The man visited her with the dawn and fed her treats and spoke softly... and then the box was moving again under a clear African sky.

* * * * *

The door was opening behind her. She gingerly edged back, one insecure step at a time, fearful that the ground would open up and swallow her whole. She looked around. The Earth under her feet felt the same but everything else had changed. People, many people, thronged the walls and rocks. They seemed to be waiting for something. They were looking at her.

The gate in the wall was open. She walked to the brink, looking out. A strange, half-remembered land stretched before her. No road. No houses. A long horizon.

One more step and she would be free. But it didn't seem right. Let them wait.

* * * * *

A score of moons or more would pass. Each day she went to the edge, the place where one more step would change her reality forever. And each time she stood and looked and watched – and retreated.

The crowd had thinned. A handful, the faithful, remained, patiently watching.

And then, one day, her foot made its mark on unbroken soil. A huge, round, crenelated, disc left its unique imprint, part of a track, her track, which left the gate and the people behind.

Without fear, she reclaimed her true home and, as the months passed, rediscovered her own kind. She was an elephant child no more and, in time, gave birth to an elephant child of her own.

* * * * *

Life is about opportunities and chances. This elephant, Tembo, was given the opportunity and took her chance. And though she lives no more, in the end, she had a life worth living. Her story is one that signifies that nothing is permanent, everything can change. Sometimes change can be for the better.

Will Travers OBE is Executive President and Co-Founder of Born Free. In 1984, he started the Born Free Foundation alongside his parents, Bill Travers MBE and Virginia McKenna OBE. Will is a regular contributor to national and international press publications, radio and TV and other media. He was awarded an OBE for services to conservation and animal welfare in the Queen's Birthday Honours in June 2012. Will is also President of the Species Survival Network and Born Free USA. He helped create the Great Ape Survival Partnership, is a Fellow of the RGS, and a member of the IUCN SSC Reintroduction Specialist Group.

35

RESPECT FOR ALL LIFE

Shubhobroto Ghosh

Memories have a strange way of connecting with people. My most potent memories of connecting with wildlife and animals have shaped the rest of my life. Observing a captive Black Kite in our school campus first gave birth to the question regarding the nature of the name 'pariah kite' at the time, given that 'pariah' is a loaded term with human connotations not associated with wild birds themselves.

There were memories of watching wild Small Indian Mongooses running around piles of wood in a storeroom in school, as well as watching Pied Wagtails in our school field. Hours and hours spent poring though books in the local library honed my connection with wildlife, especially captive animals, whose plight I identified with more than wild animals at that age.

Indian writers like Gopal Chandra Bhattacharya, Ratan Lal Brahmachary, Billy Arjan Singh and Ram Brahma Sanyal entranced and enchanted me alongside writers writing in English like Carl Sagan, Richard Feynman, Isaac Asimov, Gerald Durrell, Bernhard Grzimek and Jane Goodall. Television programmes on wildlife made by David Attenborough, Jeremy Cherfas, Jacques Cousteau and Peter Scott made a deep impression on me. There were inevitable visits to Alipore Zoo in Kolkata with my extended family and those visits introduced me to an animal that has been the focus of my interest in biology for the rest of my life for both humans and animals. The animal was named 'Cubanacan', the hybrid of a male lion and a Tigon (hybrid of a male tiger and a female African lion).

The Litigon, named 'Cubanacan' by Jose Lopez Sanchez, the erstwhile Cuban Ambassador to India, grew up to be one of the world's largest big cats of the time, weighing around 363 kg, a record 3.5 m long and 1.32 m wide at the shoulders and was recorded in the Guinness Book of Records in 1985 as the largest big cat in captivity. However, this second-generation hybrid was forgotten in subsequent publications.

Cubanacan the Alipore Zoo Litigon was born after 15 years of hybridisation attempts that started in 1964 in Kolkata. Alipore Zoo reportedly produced its first hybrid big cat, a Tigon called Rudrani, on 13 October 1972, in the sixth litter of a female African lion, Munni, and a male tiger, Munna. A second Tigon, Rangini, was born on 8 March 1974, in the same zoo. Rudrani was subsequently mated with a male lion called Debabrata, and gave birth to Cubanacan, the only surviving Litigon in a litter of three babies.

With the birth of five Litigons, Cubanacan being the most famous, Alipore Zoo in Kolkata became the only zoo in India to have Tigons and the only in the world to have successfully bred Litigons.

Cubanacan, the Litigon, died on 12 April 1991. Apart from the formidable Cubanacan, there were other Litigons in Alipore Zoo, whom I recall quite vividly: Merina and Piyali were extremely beautiful creatures. Subsequently, Alipore Zoo made several attempts to create more novel hybrids of big cats by breeding Litigons but they remained unsuccessful.

These experiments on experimental hybridisation of big cats were prohibited in India in 1985 and such banning efforts are also underway in USA and throughout the world today. The points in favour of banning hybridisation in captive hybrid cats are easy, logical, beguiling and widely believed.

However, a careful study will show us that hybridisation liaisons have taken place in the wild too. Researchers at Texas A&M University in USA and Pontifícia Universidade Católica do Rio Grande do Sul in Brazil have come a step closer to understanding the rich evolutionary history of the cat family. In a paper, featured on the cover of *Genome Research* journal in January 2016, the researchers constructed extensive family trees of the 38 cat species, which illustrated maternal, paternal, and biparental lineages within the cat family. Surprisingly, they found that lineages are not completely linear. Instead, this study revealed that feline ancestry has been shaped throughout its evolutionary history by hybridisation.

In 2008, the Magdeburg Zoo in Germany willfully killed three hybrid tiger cubs (hybrid between two purported subspecies) and I tried my best to highlight this incident in front of the world on the ground that it was wrong to kill healthy animals on the basis of genetic make-up alone. It is one thing to have a notion of desirability of creating hybrid animals in captivity that would not have come into existence if their parents had not been confined, however, it is another contention to say that healthy hybrid offspring like the Magdeburg Zoo mixed-origin hybrid animals be consciously killed on account of their genetic origin they did not choose.

Increasingly, evidence is being uncovered to show how profoundly hybridisation has influenced the natural evolution of animals as diverse as butterflies, sharks, finches, sea turtles, parrots, dolphins, bears, elephants, old-world primates or even modern humans. Modern human evolution has been shaped by our interbreeding with our cousins, Neanderthals and Denisovans, so in a way, we are all hybrids.

My connection with wildlife is most deeply guided by the Indian philosophy of 'respect for all life', which is ingrained in Article 51(A) (g) of the Indian Constitution that states it shall be the fundamental duty of the citizens of India to protect and improve the natural environment, including forests, rivers, lakes and wildlife and have compassion for all living creatures.

Working for the welfare and improvement of lives of captive zoo animals with inspiration drawn from the likes of luminaries like Gerald Durrell, Virginia McKenna, Rob Laidlaw, Jordi Casamitjana, Phil Wollen, Kailash Sankhala and Stefan Ormrod is the cardinal component of my work to help our fellow creatures.

One important book that has helped me in my endeavours to improve the condition of wild animals in captivity is *The Last Great Wild Beast Show*, by Bill Jordan and Stefan Ormrod. An intrinsic part of my work also includes efforts to raise awareness on cruelty involved in pure silk production that involves the killing of hundreds and thousands of Silkworms and Silk Moths and exploits slave labour – as revealed in a recent documentary.

Trying to put an end to elephant rides and tackling wildlife in entertainment and wildlife trade as part of my role as Wildlife Projects Manager at World Animal Protection in India, as well as fostering goodwill by sharing thoughts with compassionate environmentalists and writers like Kate Stephenson, the world over, forms the crux of my connection with wildlife today. It is my sincere hope that my contribution to this book, a noble endeavour undertaken by my colleague, Kate, will help spread the message of kindness to humans and non humans alike.

Shubhobroto Ghosh is a former journalist with *The Telegraph* whose work has also been published in *The Statesman, Times of*

India, New York Times, The Hindu, Montreal Serai, BBC, Sanctuary Asia, Saevus, Down to Earth, SciWri Club, Science Reporter and *Nature India* online. He is the former coordinator of the Indian Zoo Inquiry project sponsored by Zoocheck Canada and has attended the Principles and Practice Training course at Durrell Wildlife Conservation Trust in 1999. He did his Masters thesis on British zoos at the University of Westminster in 2004. He has worked at the Wildlife Trust of India, TRAFFIC India and is currently Wildlife Projects Manager in India for World Animal Protection in India. He has contributed to several books, including *The Jane Effect*, a biographical tribute to Jane Goodall by Marc Bekoff and Dale Peterson, *Thirty Three Ways to Look at an Elephant*, edited by Dale Paterson and an environmental biography of the ex Prime Minister of India, *Indira Gandhi : A Life in Nature* by Jairam Ramesh. He is the author of the book *Dreaming in Calcutta and Channel Islands*, published in 2015.

36

THE TIGERS' STORY

Kate Cohen

It's our planet too;
Prowling through forests is what we do…

We're majestic and strong, the biggest of cats!
We're pure muscle and fur and not at all fat;
The forests and grasslands of Asia are home,
We mark out our territory and live all alone.

Our beautiful stripes allow us to hide,
Like fingerprints they are one of a kind.
We cool off in pools, we do like a swim
Our roar's mighty loud, a bit of a din.

Despite our size we are super swift,
To run like the wind is our greatest gift.
We only eat meat and go hunting at night
Deer, antelope, pigs, we'll give them a fright.

We lie in wait, getting ready to pounce
When they get closer, it's ready, set, bounce;
We will kill our prey with a single bite
Our strength and prowess means there is rarely a fight.

We're such an iconic and beautiful beast
Drawing tourists and money, to the Far East.
But the number of tigers is falling so fast
The chances to save us have nearly passed.

For years we were seen as a hunter's best prize,
Men craving trophies, ensured our demise.
For medicine too we've been hounded and chased,
Was it really worthwhile or just a big waste?

As forests are cleared so our homes disappear,
There's so few of us now, so please shed a tear.
More tigers are living in zoos than are wild;
Stop us becoming a myth, instead make us smile.

There's only a few of us left on the planet,
Help save our homes so we don't have to panic.
We deserve a home outside of the zoo
After all, it's our planet too!

Kate Cohen is the founder of 'It's Our Planet Too', a website aimed at children to raise awareness of the environment, particularly the plight of endangered animals. It's essentially an education resource, full of fascinating facts, images, fun stuff to download and quotes as well as stories about the animals, written in rhyme. Check out: itsourplanettoo.co.uk

37

INTERACTIONS IN THE WILD WORLD

Sergio Lang

There are countless ways to experience nature. We can stroll through parks, nature preserves, and wildlife refuges and feel a sense of peace and serenity away from the hustle and bustle of urban life. We can also immerse ourselves in the wild of the mountains, the desert, even underwater, which can sometimes lead to wildlife encounters that we can never forget. Wildlife viewing is part of the excitement of stepping outside. Encountering any animal can be an incredible experience, and seeing a predator like a mountain lion, bear, or snake can be an especially thrilling and memorable experience, as long as we are educated and prepared about how to react.

In order to interact with nature safely, we must learn to be respectful of wildlife and to give wild animals space. Many species are vilified and misperceived as dangerous for just doing what comes naturally to them. When an animal attacks, it is usually because the animal is startled, feels threatened or is defending its territory. Millions of years of evolution have conditioned animals to develop these behaviours. Large predators like tigers, bears and hippos are highly territorial, and their instinct is to defend their space from intruders.

Mothers are especially protective of their young. Sadly, this can be fatal for humans and animals alike. Wildlife officials often euthanise animals that have attacked a human, on the basis that they might do it again. It is in the best interest of people and wildlife that we understand why these negative interactions occur, so they can be prevented.

A confluence of factors can contribute to animal attacks. Human developments are infringing into more and more rural areas, which contributes to habitat loss; which, in turn, places people into direct contact with large, territorial predators like wolves and mountain lions. In some parts of the world, humans have decimated the natural populations of wild prey such as wildebeest and deer, which drives predators into urban areas looking for food. They might be attracted to garbage, livestock, or even pets. People have also been found approaching wild animals, trying to get the perfect photo or simply to get a closer look, which is a mistake.

Although wild animals can be dangerous, attacks are actually quite rare. A study published in the journal of *Wilderness and Environmental Medicine* reported an average of just 157 deaths from animal attacks in the U.S. each year. A subsequent study reported that a high percentage of those fatalities were caused by farm animals and dogs.

Humans are far more deadly to animals than animals are to us. The Humane Society of the United States reports that hundreds of thousands of wild animals in the U.S. and around the world are killed by hunters each year, with hardly any connection to conservation funding or invasive species management. According to the World Wide Fund for Nature's 2020 Living Planet Report, the average size of wildlife populations declined by 68% between 1970 and 2016. Habitat loss, climate change, and pollution are driving our planet's sixth mass extinction event.

Safe experiences in the natural world are essential to reinforcing a global conservation ethic that will help to prevent further losses in biodiversity. When visiting natural areas, we must remember that we are guests and give wild animals their space. Don't approach animals or give them food, which conditions them to expect food from people. According to the National Park Service, this can lead to aggressive behavior, and ultimately to the animal being euthanised if it is deemed a threat to public safety.

Rather than be fearful of wild animals, our best defence is to remain calm, keep a safe distance, and be prepared. Depending on the situation, that might mean playing dead, making loud noises, or simply moving slowly away from the animal. It's important to do your research and familiarise yourself with the best methods for avoiding an animal attack in whatever part of the world you're lucky enough to be exploring.

Sergio Lang is the founder and CEO of NSE Global: an environmental advocacy company focused on global solutions. Sergio was born in San Diego, California, and grew up in a bilingual household in Northern Virginia. He was inspired to start NSE Global because of the growing environmental problems in our world, and he recognises the timing is critical to identify global solutions to combat these issues and protect our planet. He saw an urgent need for a platform that compiles factual information into one source to share with fellow environmental advocates.

38

THE 'TOUGH AS OLD BOOTS' CONSERVATIONIST

Kate Stephenson

Never try to outrun a lion. That was the advice jokingly stuck inside the book of goodbye messages my brother had given me for my 18th birthday.

Moving slowly under the African sun, I trod down unfamiliar terrain full of crisp, spikey shrubs and hidden potholes, and wondered how the hell I would even try to run in these things, anyway. Brownish green hiking boots weighed my feet down with each clumsy step and gave me unbearable blisters. Useless. And I was stuck with them for three and a half months; a miserable thought as I waded through the foliage towards an unsuspecting pride of lions.

I watched with baited breath as our guide's hand signals changed: Stop. Get low. Wow, we were literally going to creep up on these guys! Inching closer, I heard one of our team gasp… we'd completely overlooked a muscular adult female lounging a few feet away from the others! Through the long grass she sat poised, eyes fixed upon us, ears twitching under the pesky buzz of flies. I swallowed hard and thought to myself once more: 'Never try to outrun a lion.'

In London the rain has this irritating way of beating down diagonally; reaching in under your umbrella and touching your face, your hair, your neck. Fortunately, I don't mind the rain too much – and on a day like today, it serves only to drum up more passion. Not even sheet rain can dampen the fire in our bellies. A collective of thousands, we've descended on Hyde Park to assemble, to speak passionately about our native wildlife and the dreadful decline of natural diversity on Britain's shores. It's the People's Walk for Wildlife and together we're making a stand.

Through London's concrete jungle we march. Past Green Park, alongside Trafalgar's majestic lions and towards our Whitehall goal, the throng of conservationists trundles on. We step to the sound of birdsong, singing out not from our winged allies, but from the mobile phones of my fellow marchers. It's a sorry state of affairs, but it makes our point vividly. It's a long, slow walk to Westminster and I'm glad I'm wearing my sturdy, waterproof boots.

At 18 years old it took me a while to adjust to such a vastly different continent, but several weeks of raw and unforgiving African bush has a way of forcing you to find your feet. I was lucky enough to encounter lions many more times during my trip, including one unforgettable day we trekked at dusk. As night-time cloaked the savannah our lion pride found their voices. Tonight was a night for hunting and the anxious energy in the air was palpable.

The spine-tingling low rumble of lions called out from the distance. As the heavens opened we saw it as a sign to get out of nature's way. All around us the wild was stirring, and even us intrepid travellers had no place in it.

The heavy rain brought with it the distinct smell of Africa's dirt, and as I stepped back up onto the Land Rover I noticed the perfect imprint of the sole of my boot, filling up with precipitation. It was then I realised my muddy boots were becoming my ally – and fortunately, I don't mind the rain too much.

At 28 years old I've learnt that not everyone understands the magical smell of Africa's dirt; that birdsong is not a necessity to everyone, and that votes have more value than the trembling force of the wild.

I've learnt that in Australia the red dirt of the outback never truly washes out. I ripped one half of my shoelaces clean off somewhere near Alice Springs where you find the unlikely sight of wild camels a regular occurrence.

In St Lucia I learnt the value of packing the right equipment for a rainforest hike: a half decent pair of binoculars, compass, plenty of water and a good pair of boots.

In Norfolk I learnt that even my local wildlife is not safe from persecution. I took a chunk out of the sole of my right boot when I tripped over a tree root in the dark.

One rainy day outside Downing Street I learnt that even with an army behind you it's hard to get change-makers to listen. That, like my boots, even wild spaces have a shelf life. I learnt that in the years since first knotting the fresh new laces of my brownish green footwear, as many as 75,000 badgers have been executed on flimsy reasoning.

But most importantly, I learnt that a lion's roar in the night-time can echo in your heart for a lifetime and that in the years to come and lands unknown, I can stand tall as a conservationist, with ever-growing wisdom, and a trusty old pair of boots.

Kate Stephenson is a writer and blogger. For 10 years she has run the wildlife blog *Kate on Conservation*. She has worked for numerous media organisations specialising in children's education, such as *National Geographic Kids, Discovery Education, Channel 4 Learning, Channel 4 Talent, BBC Blast* and *BBC*

Norfolk. She is a trustee of Born Free Foundation and founder of The Wildlife Blogger Crowd; a collective of wildlife and eco-content creators, spanning online bloggers, social media curators, podcasters, film-makers and more.

39

NATURE, OUR NEIGHBOUR

Monica Kaur Bhatia

*Neighbours, we all have them; to the left, to the right, behind our house
and opposite
– if you live in a flat they may be below or on top of it.
They're up and down your road, practically everywhere,
so how come we forget about the closest ones; whose spaces we share?
These neighbours come by so sparsely, you may forget they are there,
but when they do show up, we must show that we care.*

*These neighbours have a room that's right at the back,
of which the ceiling is blue, and sometimes black.
The carpet over there isn't woolly and cream,
but dewy, cool, and a lush shade of green.
The walls of this room, instead of cement and bricks,
are a barrier of wood that is cut into sticks.
Also, these rooms have furniture too,
just like all good rooms should do;
The sofas are shrubs made not of feathers; but leaves,
and bunk beds, not of mattresses, but branches on trees.
Portraits of flowers are not hung on the walls all around,
but are 3D, scented, and sprout from the ground.*

*We think nature is distant, something far and lone,
when that couldn't be any farther from the truth, since we share the same home.*

***

As our lush Earth has been changed through the years, the string that connects us to nature has been stretched so far that it is beginning to fray – if we keep pulling, it will snap in two.

It's heartbreaking, that this weakened relationship hasn't come from mutuality: from simply cohabiting and ignoring each other, but this relationship has been weakened because the partner with a voice has been cruel to the one that does not speak. The partner with cruel intentions has misled and mistreated the one that is not only sinless, but innocent.

Our bond with nature started as such a kind friendship, in which we would water our sacred plants, and harvest ethically for survival and not greed. Over time, as many relationships do, our coupling with nature turned toxic, in which we turned from sympathising with the fact that nature doesn't fight back, to playing on that 'weakness'. We took too much, we interrupted too many – the world was more than wide enough for the both of us, yet that was so hard for us to believe. This is where I would like to emphasise: humans are not smarter than animals. Not in the slightest. Our brains develop faster, but not wiser.

As Sir David Attenborough rightly said: "It's really very unfair that man should have chosen the gorilla to symbolise all that is aggressive and violent, when that's the one thing that the gorilla is not and that we are."

We have been stupid and selfish, but our frayed relationship is still hopeful. We can grab onto the loose strands of nature we still have, we can cling onto nature; our friend and our neighbour.

There are so many ways to make it up to nature, to say sorry, and to rebuild the trust. We can use our senses to discover nature's true beauty; touch the grass and admire the flora, smell the dew of the forest and listen to the birds' symphony. We can open our hearts and homes to welcome the wild back into our lives, whether this is a bird pool or a small handful of peanuts on our deck. We can take so much more care into the effects of our actions, researching the ethics of all that we do.

Looking at the news and statistics of our damage, it is easy to feel without a hope, that the damage which has been done is irreversible. But I truly believe that if we can physically and mentally try to change our ways through our actions and energies, our relationship with the wild can turn from abusive to beautiful. There is no other option. We owe it to ourselves, to the future generation, and most importantly to nature, our neighbour.

Monica Bhatia writes blogs and prose to support the vast range of campaigns she is involved with at UK Youth for Nature. As a young conservationist, she says it is a joy to be able to pursue her passion of writing, while also tackling environmental issues.

40

THE NEW YORK CITY SKYLINE

Lucy Newman

The concrete jungle where dreams are made up.

I was 14 years old, staring out of the window of JFK airport, struggling to make out the fabled buildings in the distance as we passed through on a connecting flight. My grandmother told me stories of her visit there and promised that one day I would have my turn to see those places for real. She told me how I would feel my ears pop in the elevators of the Empire State Building, buy hot dogs in Central Park and stare into the twinkling lights of Broadway. I longed to visit New York and feel the thrilling buzz of the city that had inspired so many before me.

Six years later, I boarded my flight to New York. My dreams were coming true! After years of anticipation, I was ready to explore the city that had lodged itself in my mind for so long.

Only to find… I was underwhelmed.

Why?

Because I had already seen New York.

I had seen hundreds, perhaps thousands of photographs and videos online and on television. I had researched every corner to optimise my time there. I had watched others explore the city countless times before I had even set foot in the place. I can't help but feel like this increasingly represents the world we live in: we've seen it all before.

Social media and the internet have allowed us to see the world like never before, but that comes at a price. We have lost our sense of wonder. We are never surprised; we are never amazed, because wherever we go, we have already been there on a screen.

I have discovered, however, that there are exceptions to be found, if you know where to look.

Let's fast-forward to the summer of 2019, when I embarked on my honeymoon to the western provinces of Canada. We hoped to immerse ourselves in the best that nature has to offer. True to form I meticulously planned our every move to ensure we got the most from our visit.

The trip included a two-day journey from Vancouver to Jasper National Park. The long drive eventually necessitated a petrol stop so we pulled over in a middle-of-nowhere town. I'm not even sure I'd call it a town. There was the gas station, a few houses and the odd shop. It was a hot day, so we paid up and treated ourselves to an ice cream.

Pausing from a long drive, we thought we would use the opportunity to stretch our legs, so we pulled into a dusty parking bay and took off for a quick walk. We were no more than 100 metres from the car park when my husband caught a movement out of the corner of his eye. We stood motionless, unsure of what to expect. We watched as a dark shape amidst the trees began to shift, slowly realising, we were witnessing a bear, mere metres away.

As it began to move towards the dirt track that we were standing on, my heart pounded, and I stood up on a rock, ready to make myself appear bigger should it start to approach us. As the creature crossed the road, it paused in the middle and turned to look directly at us. I was overcome with a mixture of terror and euphoria as it made its choice. Then, it calmly turned back and carried on its way, letting itself into a nearby garden.

We hardly dared move. After a few minutes, we crept back towards the car. The bear was still in the garden but seemed completely unconcerned by our presence.

No planning, no Google search and no Instagram post could ever have provided me that moment. I could never have predicted that the single most incredible wildlife encounter of my life to date, would have been at a gas station in the Canadian backcountry.

The trip kept on giving. Having walked for hours in Jasper hoping to spot a moose, we found one right by the road on the drive back to our cabin. A boat-based bear tour in Tofino took us on an unexpected diversion to see a rare sighting of an Orca in the area. We watched in amazement as we saw its fin rise up and sink below the waves, just once, before escaping our gaze.

Nature is unpredictable.

It gives us back the wonder that we have forgotten. It creeps up and surprises us when we least expect it. In a world where you have everything at your fingertips, nature is still elusive, erratic and wild, and I think that's pretty marvellous.

Lucy Newman is the creator of One Wild Thing, a blog born from a desire to share her passion for the natural world, while giving readers the tools to make a difference in helping to protect it. Lucy couples her knowledge from her university education in marine biology and oceanography – and years of immersing herself in all-things-animal – with her skills as a secondary school teacher, to communicate the "big issues" in conservation in a way that is accessible to everyone. Every posts ends with "One Wild Thing"- a small way that you can make a difference to the issue discussed. These actions are carefully selected to not need vast amounts of

money, time or expertise, or great lifestyle changes, but rather to inspire readers to get involved a little deeper and take those baby steps forward. Find out more at: onewildthing.co.uk

41

CALL OF THE WILD

Annie Macdonald

Isn't it strange that it's really only when you completely and utterly give up on things, that they actually happen? I find that it's like that with trying to connect with nature.

It's often like that when it comes to things emerging from the garden; plants that you thought had died sending up shoots when you least expect it, or the Robin that only briefly appeared a while back, now becoming a regular visitor.

It's also weird how sometimes you have to listen to your inner sense – even if it makes no sense.

So it was one evening, when I felt a distinct call to go look in the square pond, the one right outside the kitchen door (not the 'wildlife pond' specially dug into the lawn this year for wild things!). I had long given up on this square pond, it being so murky and hosting no visible life except snails. To the point of wondering whether to clear it out and start again.

But on the evening in question, peering into the dark water in the half-light, I saw what I thought was the curl of a fallen leaf. And then it moved! I followed the shape around to find it was attached to a body, a distinctly dragon-shape body – if in miniature. A Newt!

As usual, it had taken my brain a while to compute what I'd seen. Like the time a year or two ago, when I saw, emerging from the corner of the same pond (which at that time had tadpoles and frogs), what I thought was a frog's nose – except the body kept coming straight out and along, and along... until, to my astonishment, I realised it had a tail!

This time around, I was there again at 6am the next morning – and was delighted to find that the Newt was too! I was greeted once more by a curl of a tail.

The following morning, I couldn't believe my eyes: four Newts! This was early March, after all, and quite cold.

I know now that that might have been mating season for them. Even so, upon learning that, I still worried that there were not enough leaves for their eggs to be curled up in. But the Newts knew what they were doing, the frondy leaves would certainly be fine.

Or so I'm hoping, at least. Although I haven't spotted the adults again, I am touched forever that they were there – and that, somehow, I knew to go and look.

For now, I'll just have to let things take their course – seeing what I can see, and learning what I can – all the while feeling very glad of the wild things that live right outside my back door.

Annie has been gardening off and on for the last 10 years, starting in rented gardens where it's hard to do too much, and learning by trial and error. Nowadays she has her own little garden, where she aims to do many things: in subtropical jungle (Cornwall) cottage-garden style, with myriads of pots (again Cornwall style) and wild flower meadows... trouble is, it's really quite small and based in the Midlands, so not that warm! You can follow Annie's wildlife gardening diaries and discoveries over at: livingthewildlife.garden/blog

42

HOW TO CONNECT WITH NATURE ON YOUR DOORSTEP

Molly Doubleday

Nature is everywhere. It's a common misconception that you must travel to remote lands, on a perfect day, far away from human settlements, in order to really encounter 'proper' nature. The main issue is, somewhere along the line, we lost our ability to notice nature.

Worse, we forget how to connect with it. Nature is fundamental to humanity. We are all intertwined.

Today, I am going to share with you three steps that anyone can take to reconnect with nature. As we have all become more sedentary, I will demonstrate that this can be achieved in your local patch, or even in the comfort of your own home. I'll warn you now, once you start, you may become addicted...

1. Open your senses

The first step is perhaps the simplest, yet can feel the most challenging. I want you to notice nature. I want you to use all of your senses. The more you notice, the more your senses will perk up.

Incorporate this within your daily habits. Even if your days are spent primarily at home. Making tea? Why don't you spend some time looking out the window whilst the kettle boils? Let yourself take in the blue sky, the rich green of vegetation and maybe a bird or two. Over lunch, why don't you open a window, or better yet, just pop outside your door? Allow yourself to soak up the fresh smells and the touch of a gentle breeze. More invigorating than any cup of coffee...

Even in the most urban of settings, there are glimpses of wildlife. The next time you are on a paved street, look down and I am sure you will notice a wealth of life nestled within the paving slabs. Tiny beings of lichen or moss, packed full with the colour of life. Whispering encouragement to you as you pass.

The best thing about this first step is that, over time, you won't even need to try. It will become as natural as breathing. Once this is achieved, you are ready for step two.

2. Learn about your fellow creatures

So, now your senses are fully enlivened, you might naturally start wondering about these creatures that you sense all around you. Humans are curious beings after all, so start taking some time to learn.

Don't worry, no-one is expecting you to become a wildlife expert overnight! Take micro-steps. I would recommend investing in some basic wildlife ID books, or there are some great apps available, with the *Collins Bird Guide* and the *Woodland Trust* apps being some of my favourites. Get familiar with the common species, those you see every day, and you'll be surprised how quickly and easily you retain this information. Once your garden visitors all have their appropriate names, they will become that bit more charming.

One of the best ways to connect with nature is to capture these moments with your creativity. Creating a nature journal can be a wonderful experience. Fill it with hand-scribbled observations, sketches, paintings, poems or even pressed samples themselves.

3. Bring more nature into your life

This leads us to the final step. How to bring even more nature into your life. One of the easiest ways of achieving this is to encourage wildlife to visit your home. The internet is full of grand projects that can make your garden a wildlife haven. If you have the space, you can go all out and dig luxurious ponds or create towering bug hotels. If your space is more limited, then you could put out a couple of bird feeders or grow some wildlife-enticing plants in pots. To us, this is minimal. To wildlife, these resources can be the difference between life and death. Never underestimate your ability to help nature.

Beyond furnishing your own space, there are a wealth of activities that can be done slightly further afield. Many community gardens and wildlife conservation organisations welcome volunteers to help with their work. From planting trees to monitoring butterflies, the opportunities can be numerous. I hope that, as restrictions lift, people will be able to engage with these activities more and more.

For me, nature has been an invaluable source of comfort throughout this pandemic. I feel closer to my local wildlife than ever before. As people have been forced to slow down, nature has crept into our viewfinders. It is my secret hope that humanity may start valuing nature as it should. All it needed was for people to care. If this, and nothing else, comes as a result from this pandemic, it is something good for us to hold onto.

Molly Doubleday is a conservationist working for the RSPB, who shares her passion for nature on her blog *Hippy Highland Living*. Here she describes her wild life in the Scottish Highlands and writes about her endeavours to life simply and sustainably.

43

DO YOU FEEL CONNECTED?

Barry Madden

Do you feel connected? I don't mean technologically with an iPad, smartphone, Twitter and all things digital, but naturally connected and in touch with the wild side of life? There is a whole wild world out there to enjoy, but somehow it seems so many of us have become disconnected, to spend our lives in some sort of sensory vacuum. A bubble providing insulation and isolation from the outside. In our Wi-Fi-driven age, we have forgotten to look out of the window.

I'm keenly aware of the need to engage people with nature, and was fortunate to work on a *Norfolk Wildlife Trust* project aptly called 'Natural Connections'. It was designed to do precisely what it says: connect people with the natural world, or rather reconnect them with something they had forgotten about and lost.

The essence of our work was to inspire the inhabitants of two demographically diverse parishes to become actively involved with nature. We held workshops for them on wildly ranging subjects: birds, mammals, trees, plants and bats. We arranged fungi forays, pond dipping sessions, photography workshops and moth trapping sessions. And we helped teachers get their young charges involved in making nest boxes and recording what they saw on their way to and from school.

It was wonderful. In one case, the culmination of the parishioner's efforts, young and old, was the production of an illustrated booklet documenting the natural history of the area, and in the other, a series of professionally printed maps illustrating public walks around the parish. In both cases, the end results made freely available to all. The personal legacy is having made friends that still engage enthusiastically with nature, freely admitting the whole experience has changed their lives. Click! A connection has been made.

The value of taking time to stand, stare and wonder cannot be underestimated. This happy circumstance is brought into sharp focus during my volunteering duties with the Norwich Cathedral Peregrines. Here, between April and July, we are just as likely to be asked, "Which way to your Peregrines?" as "Which way to the Presbytery?". People are galvanised to take an interest in the soap opera, and are able to watch the shenanigans of the breeding falcons via a live web feed provided by the *Hawk and Owl Trust*. More importantly, they can stand in the fresh air and watch these beautiful creatures as they go about their business; witnessing in real time the speed, power and grace of these spectacular birds. Click!

It doesn't take much. I sometimes lead walks for nature novices, those who are simply curious to find out what this wildlife thing is all about. Quite often I think there is very little of interest on show, but that is looking through the eyes of someone familiar with a particular place and its everyday inhabitants. I have to step back and look instead through the eyes of others, people who have never participated in this kind of activity before. It's easy to forget that some people have never used a pair of binoculars, that some have never seen a Redshank, and that to others, simply sitting quietly in a bird hide watching nature is a totally new experience. The delight shown by one lady when she discovered how to identify a Black-Tailed Godwit in flight sticks in my mind and speaks volumes. A resounding click!

I once sat with a friend discussing times when a connection was made through our work. We agreed that the look of wonder on a child's face when they see a Swallowtail Butterfly represents a value immeasurable in materialistic terms.

Likewise, the youngsters who get so engrossed with the contents of owl pellets that you struggle to drag them away from the soggy mess in the dish; or the fascination when a scrum of young heads crowd around the contents of a pond dipping tray; or the excited chatter when something unusual like a Grass Snake or Kingfisher appears, bringing a smile to everyone's face – making all the planning and stress so, so worthwhile. The clicks are audible.

People who are engaged in any form of education will seldom know whether their efforts have sparked a real interest, whether they have ignited something that grows over time to become a passion in their charges. Every iconic naturalist, from Audubon to Attenborough, Darwin to Durrell, was inspired by someone at some point.

My own inspiration came when I was lifted up by a chum's father to peer into the smooth mud cup of a Song Thrush's nest. There, shining back at me, were four orbs of the most brilliant blue I had ever seen. Eggs: radiant and iridescent. The colour pierced my eyes and bore into my nine-year-old mind. For weeks afterwards the only thing that mattered was those dazzling sky-blue eggs, out of sight, out of reach and all the more tantalising for it. That 10-second experience would lay the foundations for the path my life would take. A simple boredom-easing activity by a friend's dad resulted in me engaging in a lifetime of natural connection. That man never had the slightest inkling of the effect that episode had on me. I probably never saw him again; I certainly cannot recall his or my friend's name, or even what they looked like. But I can, even now, recall the wonder of seeing something wild and precious. One way or another, I've been trying to help others connect ever since. Click, click, click!

Barry Madden is Norfolk born and bred. Although birds are his first love, Barry delights in all manner of wild creatures and wild spaces – butterflies and moths are also particular favourites, with dragonflies and bees following closely behind. Aside from actually observing wildlife, he likes to photograph it and keeps busy by writing wildlife themed articles for various magazines. Read more of Barry's connections with wildlife over at: wingsearch2020.com

44

WHERE I WANT TO BE

Kate Fox

My somewhat feral upbringing on a pedigree dairy farm in the UK has shaped my knowledge and love of the natural world – and it has shaped my desire to change how people see and interact with animals, too.

I had a shamelessly 'Gerald Durrell' childhood, with hamsters in the doll's house, rabbits in the pram and newts in the basin. This unconventional life means I have never been burdened by modern-day thinking, which sees animals as slimy, creepy or disgusting.

Although my endless parade of pets and rescued animals were tolerated, my childhood efforts to turn vegetarian were greeted with dismay and embarrassment.

Without the encouragement and support to explore more suitable careers with animals, I gravitated to the familiar and went into organic grass-based dairy farming with my husband.

While I loved looking after and spending time with the cows, I somehow managed to square away the horrors of sending male calves away to be reared for slaughter. Instead, choosing to be absent when they were collected and accepting that the system was unchangeable.

I now look back on what my daughter would call 'willful ignorance' with a mix of shame but also understanding. It is so easy for all of us to look the other way and shape our lives through the lens of previous generations. However, my own weakness and failings have created understanding for those finding their way in a world where animal exploitation is the norm.

Many years down the line, I have taken the steps to become a vegan. It has been a long journey filled with family disapproval and personal judgement, but I'm finally where I want to be.

Going undercover in Vietnam's illegal bear bile trade was a defining experience for Kate Fox. The ensuing battle to free Boo the Bear and friends led to a switch from conservation photography, filming and writing to founding a charitable organisation known as Verify Humanity. Verify Humanity is a place where conservation and animal welfare meet and conventions are challenged. Kate believes that if we are to break free of a world where animal extinctions, climate change and pandemics are the norm, we need to care about the animals we protect.

45

NATURE GIVES BACK

Sally-Ann Smurthwaite

It began in January. Searing pain in my hip and leg; a sensation like nothing I had experienced before. Within a few weeks I was bedbound for days at a time. It felt like the things that mattered to me most had been stolen from me.

The shortest walk from my doorstep looping round the nearby lake is about a mile. I could barely walk a quarter of it before insidious aching curled into my hip and knee joints. Then fear and anxiety took over.

By Easter, even with lockdown in full swing, things felt more positive as physiotherapy was helping; but working from home introduced me to a more debilitating agony. Tendonitis. Unable to write, work, or even hold a book to read, the darkness overwhelmed me again. I was lost.

But we had our daily, government-permitted, allotted hour of outdoor time, and nature was patiently waiting for me there.

It began with short walks to the nearest bench stalked by discomfort. I absorbed it all: a clearing of trees, bramble, and unkempt meadow; the Chiffchaffs that chaffed their soundtrack, intertwined with Blackbird and Robin melodies; Greenfinches wheezing. The only moment I truly felt alive that day, my spirits lifted higher.

Day by day, the walks got longer. Bench hopping, I punctuated each 100-metre stretch with rest, in response to my quivering muscles and joints begging for respite. I used to eat up the distance whilst looking out for fleeing wildlife. This new method of stilted travel taught me how to sit and watch.

I always thought I had a connection with nature, but now I discovered what that truly meant. In a surreal time where I drifted on pain-laced waves, nature became my anchor. I watched the leaves transition from the rich emerald of summer into the flame hues of autumn. The ivy-coated oaks and scruffy hawthorn became intimate friends.

As did the Grey Heron, the undisputable king of the lake. Once, I caught him swooping high over the rhines, letting out a dinosaur call. I realised I had never heard that sound before. I learnt if you didn't alight your gaze directly on the heron, he would let you pass by quite close without launching himself into the air. This king demanded respect.

My daily forays became much more than the allotted hourly exercise. I became dependent on it, and it became a form of medication.

Lockdown had us physically isolating from our loved ones. Being in chronic pain is another kind of isolation, though. Most people cannot fully understand; they sympathise, but then they move on. It put immense pressure on my relationship with my partner and I felt friends withdraw.

While the human world was falling away, I forged new connections. A world filled with fascinating individuals who expected nothing of me. They were happy to live their lives around me.

One early summer evening, darkness encroaching, a numbness settled over me. There is only so much despair the brain can handle. When a flickering black shape shot across my periphery. I looked out the window; a bat! Then another! I crossed the room and sat on the floor, my nose pressed against the glass. Eyes wide in the dark, the bats flitted around our oak trees, zigzagging the garden perimeter. Close enough that I could make out the shapes of their wings in glimpses. I focused on the bats, waiting for the next sighting and the next. Fully in the moment, my entire focus flying through the night with these strange creatures.

Over the summer we watched the Canada Geese goslings grow. They formed a nursery 30 goslings strong, guided by their parents. We would sit among the flocks grazing on the banks. We also saw the arrival of the resident mute swans' cygnets. The male became shockingly aggressive towards the goslings. New dramas unfolded every day. Consumed by their lives, I forgot the trials of my own.

This time autumn was different, formerly a fair-weather explorer, this was usually when I went into hibernation. Now able to walk the whole lake without stopping, with my body getting stronger, I made a promise to myself that I would walk the lake every single day.

I was rewarded for my dedication. On a bleak morning, I walked over the bridge and gave a cursory glance into the rhine below. There was a sudden strange quacking-grunt hybrid sound of alarm. I glimpsed a flash of white fish belly in a narrow-curved beak, then red-brown feathers, which sat brushed back upon her head. She had a gleaming silver back.

My heart thundered with the thrill of a new sighting – or perhaps it was some kind of innate primal warning, triggered by the sudden movement of a wild animal. I sped to the other side of the bridge to see the bird that had fled. A female Goosander.

The pain took so much away. But nature gave something back.

Sally-Ann Smurthwaite is an environmentalist and writer living in Cardiff. She studied an MSc in Environment, Science and Society at University College London, before embarking on a full-time

career in the environment sector. Alongside this, Sally runs *Wild and Green* blog and documents her own adventures living in South Wales over at *Sally by the Sea*.

46

NATURE'S EFFECTS ON THE HUMAN BODY

Sergio Lang

Take a moment and imagine yourself in a natural setting. Use all your senses. Imagine inhaling the clean, fresh air and the scent of evergreen trees. Feel the warmth of the sun on your skin. Hear the birds chirping and branches swaying overhead. Look off into the distance and see the endless shades of green over the rolling hillside.

Now picture a different setting: a busy city at rush hour. Cars are lined up next to you, inching forward and honking their horns. The smell of exhaust fills the air. You're surrounded by the dull colours of concrete, steel, and asphalt. It's easy to spot the differences between these two settings, but the effects on the human body aren't always as obvious.

Nature's positive impact on human health has been documented in modern literature for many years. In the 1800s, the writer Henry David Thoreau described the calming effect of nature; naturalist John Muir reported how wilderness soothed the nerves of urban residents; landscape architect Frederick Law Olmstead believed parks had a positive impact on mental health. Indigenous peoples have appreciated the therapeutic properties of nature for thousands of years.

Over the past century, even while nature has been progressively exploited by humankind, the evidence connecting nature to human health has grown. Time spent in and around nature has been linked to improved cognition, reduced stress, and increased self-esteem.

In a recent study by Martin et al. (2020), the authors determined that visiting nature at least once a week is associated with better health, happiness, and well-being. In a study published in 2010, Rodney H. Matsuoka observed 101 public high schools and found that views of green vegetation were significant factors in academic performance and graduation rates. In a number of studies, views of the natural world have been associated with higher scores in reading, language proficiency, and maths (Selhub and Logan, 2012).

Nature's positive impacts on human health are not limited to the brain. In a landmark study published in 1984, environmental psychologist Roger Ulrich found that patients who were able to gaze out their hospital window at a garden healed faster from surgery, infections and other ailments. The patients with a view of trees healed, on average, a day faster, needed less pain medication, and had fewer post-surgical complications compared to patients who saw a brick wall out their window. It's possible the garden view helped reduce patient stress, which can improve immune system function and speed up the healing process.

Nature may even help us live longer. In a study by James et al. (2016) of more than 100,000 women over a period of eight years, green vegetation was associated with decreased mortality. Using satellite imagery to measure levels of vegetation, and looking at issues such as kidney and respiratory diseases and cancer, the researchers found that women living in greener areas had a 12% lower death rate. The study suggests that the mental health benefits, increased opportunities for social engagement and physical activity, and lower exposure to air pollution, all of which are correlated with access to nature, play an important role in life expectancy. According to the European Environment Agency, every 10% increase in green space is associated with a reduction in diseases equal to an increase of five years' life expectancy.

Through decades of scientific research, it is well established that nature provides psychological, cognitive and physiological benefits. One of the most remarkable things is that even small "doses" of nature, such as a few minutes spent outdoors, a view through a window, a photo of a landscape, indoor plants, or even watching a documentary film about nature, can positively influence human health (Keniger et al., 2013). More research is still needed, however, into other subject areas, related to the multisensory effects of immersing in nature, as well as the social and spiritual benefits.

So how can we apply this research to improve our own lives? According to environmental psychologist Adina Deacu, "Take some time off any time you have the opportunity and spend it in natural settings, even if it's in the small park around the corner of your apartment or office. Just make sure to protect nature and don't leave any garbage behind you wherever you might choose to go. It is in each of us to protect natural landscapes for the psychological comfort they provide, if not for the whole global warming dilemma." (Why Are We So Attracted to Natural Environments?)

Sergio Lang is the founder and CEO of NSE Global; an environmental advocacy company focused on global solutions. Sergio was born in San Diego, California, and grew up in a bilingual household in Northern Virginia. He was inspired to start NSE Global because he recognises the timing is critical to identify global solutions to combat these issues and protect our planet. He saw an urgent need for a platform that compiles factual information into one source to share with fellow environmental advocates.

47

LOCKDOWN NATURE

Lisa Stubbings

Photographs can evoke all sorts of emotions. To me, the essence of being a wildlife and nature photographer is the ability to capture the beauty of a subject situated in its own environment, to treasure it and relive the feelings it provides.

I was asked recently what wildlife photography meant to me, and if there's one thing that the time spent in lockdown and shielding during this awful pandemic has afforded me, it's the opportunity to reflect on that.

Feeling alienated from the rest of the humanity – owing to the fact that I possess more autoimmune diseases than you can count on one hand – the pandemic seemed to highlight that nature is everywhere, it is all around us.

To be outside amongst such beauty has a calming and soothing effect – I personally find nature photography to be very therapeutic; the everyday stresses, illnesses and challenges of life seem to ebb away when I'm outside with my camera.

I found great solace in my hobby, when I suffered from a devastating family bereavement. Being outdoors gave me time to think and time to connect with the world around me. I am lucky enough to live very close to a river, where I would spend many hours contemplating and listening to the gorgeous melody of birdsong.

Nature is so thought-provoking, natural world photography promotes conservation and preservation. To be able to cherish what we have, to breathe fresh air and to be able to feel the warmth of the sun, is something I will never tire of. I find it promotes my general self-worth and mental well-being.

As you can imagine, being stuck indoors for months on end was a struggle. Nature was so close that I could see it, but sadly I was not able to embrace it.

To me, photography means to be at one with nature. To have the opportunity to be able to experience a sentient being, in its natural habitat, is truly something to behold. To be able to glimpse the stunning amber pelage of a fox, the statuesque outline of a hare, a sparkling flash of blue from a darting Kingfisher and to admire the stunning beauty of a deer, is an exhilarating and fantastic feeling, a timeless and cherished memory.

So, as we are now allowed to ease slowly out of lockdown, after so many devastating losses, let's not ruin the quietness and the beauty that surrounds us. Nature has thrived without being disturbed during this time, it's remained at peace without the threat of man.

Lisa Stubbings is an aspiring nature and wildlife photographer, capturing the beauty of the natural world. Her blog, The Fox Den, can be found over at: freeworldpress905.wordpress.com

48

SHINING TREES

Nick Stephenson

Something on the telly made you cry
And I don't even think I'd like to know
Is it all about your fantasies
Or lying on a bed under shining trees

Oh it's so crazy, that beauty can look that way
And the emotion comes out when the news kicks in
And if you let me call back the joy that you fought so hard to win

Back to the shining trees
Back to the shining trees

Something in the music made you dance
Dance like a child, a child of grace
You can walk away, it's OK
You can fly away, fly away

Oh it's so crazy, that beauty can look that way
And the emotion comes out when the news kicks in
And if you let me call back the joy that you fought so hard to win

Back to the shining trees
Back to the shining trees

'Shining Trees' is the lyrics to a song of the same name, by Nick Stephenson.

Nick Stephenson's wildlife storytelling takes the form of music; he is a singer-songwriter with a passion for nature and wildlife. His playlist 'Songs of Nature' is available to listen to on Soundcloud.

He released a fundraising single 'Poor Little Boy' in 2019 for One Man's Rescue campaign, which provides senior dogs in rescue centres with fun days out. Find out more at: nickfstephenson.com

49

A TALE OF HOPE, IN A WORLD FULL OF FEAR

Kate Stephenson

"Tell us again, Mum, tell us about the time when we were little and humans gave the world back to the animals. Tell us about how it saved the rivers, and the trees, and the giants of Africa, and the tiny bees in our garden."

"Well, we didn't exactly *give* it back, nature made the first move. A bit a like a game of chess, I suppose. Thankfully we took nature's side, in the end."

"How did it start again, Mum? What made the people sick?"

"Greed, darlings."

"And the virus, what was it again? It began with a 'C', didn't it?"

"Co… Consumerism, dears. Needless, wasteful consumerism."

"What made the people change?"

"Well, there was once, or twice – maybe three times – when we were all had to stay in our houses. And during that time an entire year passed…"

"Oh, I love this bit!"

"Me too!"

"…In that time, we learnt how to get by without unnecessary shopping, or unnecessary car journeys.

"We learnt to look after our neighbours and appreciate that our actions can affect other people – even those that we can't see in our own streets, or towns or countries.

"We even learnt how to travel by plane less, and some of the coastlines that had been busy and full of tourists and their discarded property became havens for wildlife.

"Even waterways in canal cities became clean and undisturbed – so much so, that new, wild residents moved in.

"We saw what happened when we let places get 'overgrown', and we made a special effort to pick up old plastic from beaches. We learnt how to love the outside again, because we'd missed it so much. And we learnt how to love people, the world over – because we missed human interaction, too."

"What about the animals?

"Did we miss them, too?"

"Well my children, we finally learnt how to love them enough to let them go, to let them be free. Sure, we missed them in some ways; but we discovered that if you were respectful, and didn't disturb them, you could sometimes catch a glimpse of these wild species going about their lives. Much like we do now."

"And what about the years before that, Mum? When the pandemic happened?"

"Ah, you mean the days of the Coronavirus? You were very small then. Some say that's what started the Big Change. It created the first rumblings of a new world…"

"Was it, Mum?"

"Do you think it was?"

"I'm not sure, darlings. I can't be sure at all."

Kate Stephenson is a writer and blogger. For 10 years she has run the wildlife blog *Kate on Conservation*. She has worked for numerous media organisations specialising in children's

education, such as *National Geographic Kids*, *Discovery Education*, *Channel 4 Learning*, *Channel 4 Talent*, *BBC Blast* and *BBC Norfolk*. She is a trustee of Born Free Foundation and founder of The Wildlife Blogger Crowd; a collective of wildlife and eco-content creators, spanning online bloggers, social media curators, podcasters, film-makers and more.

50

WHEN I FINALLY LEAVE THIS PLACE

Chloé Valerie Harmsworth

When I finally leave this place
That has held me for so long
Will I be a bird of grace
Or be a bird of song?

Will I be suspended
In the air so out of reach
And when my time is ended
Will your call succeed my speech?

Shall my feet transform to claw
My blue eyes pale to white
Will I embody what I adore
With wind my new delight?

Shall my nose and mouth remould as beak
My skin and hair convert to feather
My eyes sharpen for mammals I seek
Connected to sky forever?

A symbol of strength I would become
Restored from distant history
A rare sight now known by everyone
If "you" became "me".

Your shape has brought me endless joy
As well as awe and wonder
So when my body begins to cloy
And it's time to leave it under,

Perhaps my soul will rearrange
My form as I've described
And I won't find it hard or strange
To leave the soil to which I'm tied,

And finally I will leave this place
Shedding my worthless fear
And love and hope with it replace
With you, my friend, quite near.

Chloé Valerie writes about wildlife and the environment in order to raise awareness of conservation issues and to encourage people to reconnect with nature, to benefit their mental well-being and also the world. She has written for various magazines, and writes and illustrates her own nature diary, which explores her local Hertfordshire green spaces throughout the year. She also creates artwork and takes photographs of nature, inspired by her walks. She has written a book about woodlands, due for publication in 2022. See more at: chloevalerienatureart.wordpress.com

EPILOGUE

We don't need to be scientists or botanists or even naturalists to appreciate and love nature. The beauty and complexity of the natural world is an extraordinary gift for us all to enjoy. Young and old.

This book is proof that it can take only a few words to lead us to, and be touched by, nature's magic. Some of the stories are very personal – poignant, nostalgic. Others see the world through the eyes of wild creatures. Others cherish the experience of sharing moments with a bird, a hare, an otter, an insect.

Age is of no consequence – as readers will see. Early in life or nearing the end, our hearts and minds can be opened. It is only when we see, and really understand, and truly care, that nature can survive.

As I write this I am sitting beside a Scottish loch – a scene of such beauty and tranquillity it takes your breath away. Of course, the ospreys fly overhead, and sometimes the fish are victims. But, unless you are a plant eater, that is the way of the wild, the way of survival.

A few days ago, a mother duck and nine ducklings swam over towards us. Each day I counted them and there were always nine. We sit in silence watching, and I know I will never forget their innocence, their beauty and their trust.

In this fascinating and very personal book, many of the writers have given us a glimpse of their inner beliefs; their views on those who exploit and disrespect animals; their joy as they watch insects busily exploring the verges of roads or seabirds swooping over the ocean. Maybe, what struck me most of all, was the realisation of the gratitude so many of the authors felt towards wild creatures and wild places. Is this the other side of the Covid coin?

We have had a time during 'lockdown' to watch and listen to the sights and sounds of the natural world. And now we have rediscovered its half-forgotten fascination, and the joy it can bring, will we learn, change and assure a future for the wildlife world? For our children – and for the animals themselves.

It is one of the greatest hopes of my life.

Virginia McKenna
Born Free Co-Founder and Trustee
bornfree.org.uk

ACKNOWLEDGEMENTS

Taking on a project such as this – including the initial task of establishing The Wildlife Blogger Crowd community in the first place – has been an exciting challenge. At a time of such uncertainty, with limitations on physical contact, and terms like 'social distance' becoming a part of our everyday vocabulary, it has certainly been a pleasure to have the opportunity to connect with like-minded people across the globe, of all ages and walks of life – a process that has served to make me feel as though 'distance' means very little, and that 'social' is of the highest order.

As such, I must first and foremost thank the ever-growing collective of wildlife storytellers, whose knowledge and passion has both motivated and inspired me this past year. The Wildlife Blogger Crowd has proved to be a collective of compassionate, empathetic people who not only believe in progress and change when it comes to reversing the impacts of climate change and the biodiversity crisis, but who deal in action. Each time a story is a shared; a blog is published; a social media status, Tweet or caption is posted: a positive action is being taken. An action that serves to educate, to lobby, to mobilise. Good, clear communication is the lifeline that conservationists and scientists need to make their work happen; to gain government support, public support and funding through either of those channels – and every single person who has contributed to this book, or joined The Wildlife Blogger Crowd is playing their part. For that, I am immensely grateful.

Thank you to my family: my children Ada and William, whose presence inspires me to be brave – to use my pen (or keyboard, as it were) as my sword in this battle to protect nature and wildlife. To do all that I can to help provide a world in their future that's more ecologically rich than the one I have known. To my Mum and Nan especially for telling me stories of a *former* time that was ecologically richer than the one I have known, too. For making me believe that few things are ever out of reach, and that most things come back around.

Thank you to the Bradt team for guiding me through this process. This is my first experience of working on a book, and the enthusiasm and guidance from Head of Editorial, Anna Moores, has been invaluable. Thanks too, to Claire Strange, Adrian Phillips, Iona Brokenshire and Sue Cooper for their help and input into this project, and Ian Spick for his excellent design work. I have long admired the work of Bradt and this experience has only served to strengthen my respect for your work.

Thank you to Virginia McKenna, Will Travers, and Jonathan and Angela Scott, for being generous with your time, words and wisdom. Your unwavering support always humbles me.

Chloé Valerie Harmsworth, who has provided a wonderful cover design – thank you for always being just an email away. For always being a springboard to bounce thoughts and ideas off of, and for being prepared to step in and help at any given time. I'm delighted to have had the chance to work you after many years of crossing paths, and I'm excited to witness your future endeavours too.

To my husband, Nick, your support, encouragement, patience, counsel and generosity of time and emotion never goes unnoted or underappreciated – but I know you know that already.